Sorcery at Caesars

Sugar Ray Leonard (left) and Marvelous Marvin Hagler, in
1981, at the Petronelli Gym in Brockton, Mass. Each saw in
the other a big payday and a career-defining challenge.

SORCERY
AT
CAESARS

SUGAR RAY'S MARVELOUS FIGHT

STEVE MARANTZ

INKWATER
PRESS

Portland • Oregon
INKWATERPRESS.COM

www.inkwaterpress.com

ISBN-13 978-1-59299-336-9
ISBN-10 1-59299-336-2

Publisher: Inkwater Press

Printed in the U.S.A.
All paper is acid free and meets all ANSI standards for archival quality paper.

To Alison

*Knowing her fate, Atlantis sent out
ships to all corners of the Earth.*

On board were the Twelve:

*The poet, the physician, the
farmer, the scientist,*

*The magician and the other
so-called Gods of our legends.*

Though Gods they were.

Donovan

Table of Contents

· · · · · · · · · · · · · · · · · · · ·

Foreword

· ·

THE FUN BEGAN IN 1973. Or thereabouts. I was a
sports columnist for the *Boston Globe* and Marvin Hagler
was a 19-year-old boxing prodigy from Brockton, Massachusetts, a place well within the *Globe*'s circulation area,
so I was consigned to follow him for most of his long
and circuitous rise to fame, fortune, and, of course, the
middleweight title.

I first watched him work on local fight cards at high
school gymnasiums and ball fields, dance halls and func-
tion rooms, and eventually traveled with him to London,
New York, Chicago, Philadelphia, Las Vegas, a succession
of grand athletic stops. Fourteen years. Marvin wound
up in the spotlight. I wound up in four-star hotel rooms,
expense account living at its finest. Not a bad deal for
either of us.

"I'm calling from my round bed, looking at myself in
the mirror on the ceiling," I reported from a suite at Cae-

sars Palace to friends back home in the days preceding Marvin's ultimate fight on April 6, 1987, against Sugar Ray Leonard. "I think I will now step into the Jacuzzi, which is sunk into the middle of the living room floor."

The stories were very easy to write. (I used a contraption called "a typewriter," which I now describe as "sort of like a word processor, but without the need for either electricity or a printer.") Marvin was the common man doing quite uncommon things. He was without flash or guile, solid as a Sunday morning in a Baptist church. His trainers were Goody and Pat Petronelli, local Brockton guys who turned a lottery ticket into a meal ticket. He stuck with them for the entire ride, stuck with an assortment of Brockton characters that included doctors, lawyers and just plain friends.

Never did he allow himself to be packaged, put under that blister-wrap of sports promotion and hype. He began local and stayed local. There was a timeless quality about his operation, a return to the earlier boxing world of, say, the Fifties, when the Friday Night Fights were a black-and-white television staple and neighborhoods sent their worthiest contenders into the ring. He was black-and-white basic, a bald-headed, left-handed bundle of action with a very good punch and an even better chin.

He sparred with his brother. He ran his training miles in the morning in combat boots. Basic. Not a good interview, his quotes mainly were a collection of aphorisms like "Destruction and Destroy" and "I'm putting myself in jail" when he went into preparations for his next fight. He believed every one of them.

His training camp for the big fights usually was in Provincetown, Mass., on the far tip of Cape Cod. A ring was set up at the Provincetown Inn, which seemed to be an unlikely site since it catered to a gay male clientele.

"Why are you in this place?" I asked on one visit.

"I like to be out here with the sissies," Marvin replied. "Keeps my mind on my business."

Fighting anyone who was put in front of him, a collection of hard cases who mostly had been skipped as too dangerous by the carefully developed Sugar Ray and the well-connected Thomas (Hit Man) Hearns from the Kronk Gym in Detroit, Marvin forced his way into the rotation. He kept knocking down the people in front of him until he had to be taken seriously. He won so much that sound economics, not to mention the paying public, demanded Sugar Ray and Hearns had to fight him.

The entire ride was a wonder. The plots and sub-plots were constant, far removed from the familiar machinations of Boston team sports with their cyclical playoffs and draft days and salary disputes. Surprises abounded as rumors and press conferences, charges and counter-charges, ended with spectacular events, electricity running straight through the assembled bodies.

My favorite night of all was Sept. 27, 1980, when Marvin won the middleweight title at Wembley Arena in London. His opponent was Alan Minter, a well-intentioned Brit who had become a national symbol of English patriotism. He wore the design of the flag, the Union Jack, on his shorts, a reminder to his fans of his love for his country.

Many of those fans, I noticed in the lobby before the fight, seemed to be skinheads, a fearsome group covered in tattoos and black leathers, chains hanging from their tight pants. The skinheads were buying beer in bulk, full cases of the stuff, 24 bottles each, then lugging the cases into the upper reaches of the arena. I never had seen this before.

Dong. The fight began. Marvin destroyed Minter from the beginning. Dong. Cuts were opened quickly on the Englishman's face. Blood ran down to his patriotic shorts. Dong. The fight lasted only a minute and 45 seconds into the third round, stopped by the referee. Marvin finally was the champion.

The skinheads, with their 24 beers apiece, hadn't had time to consume much of the product. What to do? The bottles, full, started flying toward the ring. A riot began. The Petronelli brothers dropped Marvin to the canvas and covered him with their bodies. The people at ringside, myself included, looked for an escape. I was sitting next to Vito Antuofermo, former middleweight champion of the world, who was doing color commentary on Italian television.

"Follow me," Vito said.

I put that typewriter contraption over my head for protection. I followed. Somewhere on the trip out of the arena, fights breaking out everywhere, an unsuspecting Brit put a hand on Vito's shoulder. Just a hand. The former middleweight of the champion reacted with an immediate right uppercut to the jaw. The Brit went flying.

Hah.

· · ·

I think of this – all of this and much more – after reading *Sorcery at Caesars*. In deft, terrific prose, Steve Marantz has laid out the itineraries for Marvin and Sugar Ray, leading up to one memorable night in the desert. The whole story is here, as exciting as it was the first time. All the details return.

Makes a man want to take a Jacuzzi in the middle of his living room.

— Leigh Montville

Prologue

· · · · · · · · · · · · · · · · · · · ·

ON THE NIGHT OF April 6, 1987, Sugar Ray Leonard stole a fight. A couple of million witnesses saw him get away with it.

Leonard's theft was so slick that the victim, Marvelous Marvin Hagler, didn't know until it was too late. His middleweight title was picked clean and gone, forever.

It happened at a parking lot behind Caesars Palace Hotel and Casino, in an outdoor boxing ring, under a Nevada moon.

Hagler was supposed to win. The betting public had made him a 3-1 favorite. In a poll of 67 media experts, 60 picked Hagler to win and 52 predicted he would knock out Leonard. Hagler had not lost in 10½ years, while Leonard had fought just once in five years. A victory by Leonard was considered less likely than permanent damage to his body and mind.

After a round Leonard was unharmed and on his

feet. After two rounds, then four, then eight, Leonard reminded his doubters that boxing is more than a test of strength – it is an art, a Sweet Science. Through 12 rounds, Leonard and Hagler boxed with skill, purpose, and occasional fury. Neither scored a decisive blow, and at the final bell, Hagler raised his hands in triumph while Leonard dropped to his knees in exhaustion. Moments later only Leonard's hands were upraised.

Leonard won by a split decision. Two judges voted for Leonard, and one for Hagler. Though Hagler and untold spectators saw Hagler as the winner, only the votes of the three judges mattered. Their honesty was not in question, by most accounts, only their perception.

Leonard had sold himself to two judges, not literally, but as a salesman sells a product, a con man sells a lie, or a magician sells an illusion. More importantly, he had sold himself to Hagler, who gave him just enough respect, and room, to close the deal.

Leonard was a born salesman. He had sold boxing to an indifferent public after Muhammad Ali's era ended. He had sold beverages and food and sporting goods throughout the 1980s. He had sold an upright and amiable image of himself that was patently false. But this was Leonard's greatest snow job.

In the 1973 Oscar-winning film, *The Sting*, a wry and debonair con man played by Paul Newman swindled cash from a rough character played by Robert Shaw. In the 1987 version Leonard was Newman, Hagler was Shaw, the con was legal, and the prize was not money. It was bragging rights to an era.

Aficionados refer to boxing as the Fight Game, which is both endearing and ironic, because games are fun, and boxing is something else. One subtle use of the phrase, voiced by a Leonard loyalist, Ollie Dunlap, summarized the multi levels on which Leonard operated.

"Ray put the Fight Game on Marvin," Dunlap said.

The caper took 14 years to set up. The last 15 months were plotted in exact detail. The deed took just 12 three-minute rounds to execute.

In its own way, it was a perfect Sting.

Of course, Hagler did not see it that way.

But if winners write history, a salesman, a con, a Sweet Scientist, and a sorcerer wrote this one. Leonard was each and all in the parking lot behind Caesars.

This is the story of sorcery at Caesars, and how Sugar Ray put the Fight Game on Marvelous Marvin.

CHAPTER 1

1982: Sugar Ray Ascendant

As 1982 DAWNED SUGAR Ray Leonard was the most celebrated athlete in America. *Sports Illustrated* magazine, whose influence was at its peak, named him Sportsman of the Year for 1981. In the 27-year history of the award just one other boxer, Muhammad Ali in 1974, had won it.

SI's cover photo posed Leonard on a wing chair of plush crimson cushion and polished ornamental wood. He wore a double-breasted suit of gray twill, an off-white dress shirt, and a crimson club tie. Two rings adorned the manicured fingers of his left hand and his left leg was crossed casually over his right. A knowing half-smile creased his iconic face. The impression was one of comfort, wealth, and power, and vaguely lethal.

The magazine reported that in a recent poll asking eighth-graders whom they most admired, entertainers dominated, with Burt Reynolds at No. 1. Ranked at No.

9 was Leonard, the top-rated athlete, between George Burns and Steve Martin.

"Unquestionably, Leonard is now the strongest of modern alloys, this blend of hero and celebrity," wrote author Frank Deford.

He was classically handsome, with dark, liquid eyes, prominent cheekbones, strong jaw line, a high brow, full sensuous mouth, and a sculpted physique worthy of a Michelangelo. He moved with the grace of Astaire, and carried himself with elegance more typical of old money than a prizefighter.

His mocha-colored skin was smooth and unmarked, save for a slash over his left eyebrow, and when he flashed his "million-dollar" smile, his face erupted in dimples. He dressed so impeccably that *Playboy* magazine named him to its list of best dressers, his wardrobe an eclectic combination of Brooks Brothers, Armani, and yachting casual.

© Ollie Dunlap

Sugar Ray Leonard's "million dollar smile."

Indeed, Leonard was a nearly perfect embodiment of the pop culture zeitgeist. He seemed less a boxer than an actor playing a boxer, with his matinee idol looks and pitch-perfect ring temperament that veered between playful and vicious. For Leonard boxing was more than a collision of gloved fists, sinew, bone, and will. Boxing was theater, with character and plot, and he played it as a masquerade of deception and concealment.

There was a touch of 007 in his suave and cold appraisal.

"I can train, have lunch with you, beat you up the next day, and have lunch with you again," he once said.

The first actor elected president, Ronald Reagan, symbolized the movement of entertainment to the center of American life. "Politics is just like show business," The Gipper said. "You have a hell of an opening, coast for a while, and then have a hell of a close."

Much of 1980s popular culture reflected Reagan's optimism, Cold War ideology, and emphasis on traditional ideals of family, business, heroism, masculinity and authority. Reagan catalyzed a backlash to the cynicism and anger of the Vietnam years and conjured an America of older, simpler bedrock values. Chief among those values was wealth, a belief in its exquisite desirability and Wall Street's capacity for generating it. Among Reagan's values, this was Leonard's favorite.

In September 1982 NBC would debut a new sitcom, "Family Ties," which featured actor Michael J. Fox in the role of Alex Keaton, the teenaged Reagan-like son of hippie-era parents. The Keaton character seemed to channel

Leonard, who, on the "Tonight Show," had joked that members of his large entourage were "tax write-offs."

As Wall Street and Reaganism ascended in the early 1980s, so too did the CEO of Sugar Ray Leonard, Inc., who stood tall for free enterprise. His business model of free agency had challenged the power brokers of boxing, and his purses, which now totaled about $35.5 million, were the wonder and envy of the sporting world. Leonard's three bouts in 1981 had paid him close to $15 million. In comparison, Dave Winfield was Major League Baseball's highest paid player at about $2.3 million per year. Rich beyond his wildest dreams, Leonard lived in a gated castle with a stone turret and wine cellar in Potomac, Md.

The 1980 firing of his original trainer Dave Jacobs had opened a window on his flinty management style. The dismissal of Jacobs, who had coached him since the age of 13, Leonard said matter-of-factly, meant "one less check to write." Leonard held his payroll to 20 percent, well below the payrolls of other elite fighters. Marvin Hagler, by comparison, gave a standard 33 percent cut to his handlers. Thomas Hearns paid his manager/trainer 33 to 50 percent, while Roberto Duran hardly knew what his patrician manager took, and as a result, ended up broke.

Leonard's image was not defined by political or religious causes. In this, Leonard was the anti-Ali, as he conscientiously refused to voice an opinion on issues outside of boxing. Fifteen years earlier star athletes Jim Brown, Bill Russell, and Lew Alcindor (soon to be Kareem Abdul Jabbar) had stood behind Ali in his refusal to be drafted.

But the 1960s was a brief departure from a tradition of apolitical star athletes, personified by O.J. Simpson in the 1970s and Michael Jordan in the 1990s. Leonard's approach mirrored the relative calm of the post-Vietnam, post–civil rights era.

"Ray didn't really have political leanings," Ollie Dunlap, his administrator, recalled. "If someone talked politics he would say 'we each have our own beliefs' and leave it at that."

"If Ray wanted to support something he did it privately," recalled Michael G. Trainer, his attorney. "Some people were put off by that."

ABC's star broadcaster Howard Cosell advised Leonard on his public persona. Cosell, who had taken Leonard under his wing at the 1976 Olympics, taught Leonard to be an astute listener, and to lead conversations away from politics and religion. "Don't let them lead you," Cosell commanded.

The Nation of Islam, which drew Ali into its fold in the early 1960s, made an indirect run at Leonard, raised as a Baptist. Its followers included James Anderson, Ali's longtime bodyguard, who was hired as a security expert by Leonard in 1980. Anderson, and others, drew Leonard into discussions about Islam, but he was not enticed.

Leonard's apolitical persona extended to race. Except for once early in his career, Leonard avoided race as a topic. This, along with his clean-cut appearance and deft command of language, enabled his attorney, Trainer, to say during the build-up to his 1981 bout with Detroit's Hearns, "Ray has this special ability to make white people feel good about themselves. They like Ray and they say to themselves, 'There's a black man I like. I'm not a racist. I don't have to feel guilty.'"

African-Americans, on the other hand, were hesitant about Leonard. They suspected he had lost touch with his cultural roots; Hearns' fan base was said to increase the deeper he went into black ghettoes. Yet, African-Americans could not ignore Leonard's symbolic importance. As Deford wrote, "the image of the typical black family as a matriarchy is dented" every time Leonard and his son appeared together in a 7-Up commercial. By 1982 the Leonards were one of the most visible African-American nuclear families. Leonard was Cliff Huxtable before Bill Cosby created the character in 1984 for "The Cosby Show," the first sitcom featuring a stable, middle-class African-American family.

Soon Leonard's life would become a stage façade. After he beat Hearns in September 1981 in a spellbinding match that elevated him to Sportsman of the Year, Leonard began to change. His comments to Deford hinted at a more expansive view of himself. "You see, I don't consider myself a fighter," Leonard said. "I'm a personality."

Leonard's inner circle noticed that he spent more time away from home. In the past, he had returned to Maryland soon after he fought or worked a boxing telecast. But after the Hearns bout he began to linger in Los Angeles, where exclusive doors opened, at sleek private homes in the hills above Hollywood, and at chic nightspots where the rich and glamorous cavorted.

Ten years earlier a boxing coach had nicknamed him "Sugar Ray" because his smooth ring skills evoked the great post-war champion, Sugar Ray Robinson. The nickname gave birth to Leonard's alter ego, a willful creature of bright lights and hidden pleasures. Now, untethered from gravity, his alter ego came of age.

"That's when Ray became Sugar," said Dunlap. "He didn't want to be a world champion. He wanted to be a superstar."

In early 1982, Leonard scheduled a couple of tune-ups until a bout with Hagler or a rematch with Hearns could be arranged. Hagler, at this time, had defended his middleweight title three times, with relative ease. He was 27, in his mid-prime, and respected by aficionados for his old-school professionalism. A former construction worker, Hagler hailed from Brockton, Mass., the gritty mill town put on the map by former heavyweight champion Rocky Marciano.

Geography and sensibility stamped Hagler as blue collar. Early in his career he pushed wheelbarrows of fresh cement to make ends meet. One day he lost control of an overloaded wheelbarrow, flipped it, and had to clean up the mess. When he returned to the cement mixer, he asked for a lighter load. "Don't let these muscles fool you," Hagler said, as his co-workers roared.

To the larger public he was a bit of a puzzle, however. Though his shaved head and chiseled physique had become familiar on the ambitious young cable channel, HBO, he was rarely seen on network TV and was yet to be featured in closed-circuit theaters.

His credo, "destruct and destroy," was alliterative, catchy, and expressive of his clinical approach to may-

© Angie Carlino

Marvelous Marvin Hagler's shaved head and chiseled physique struck fear in opponents.

hem, as was his reaction to blood in the ring. "It turns me on," Hagler said. "The monster comes out."

Both intrigued and repelled, the public kept its distance. Hagler brooded over his lesser celebrity, and envied Leonard his prominence and outsized paydays. He imagined that if he defeated Leonard, those things would come to him.

In February Leonard was in Reno, Nevada, for a bout with journeyman Bruce Finch. He kissed towels monogrammed with his initials and threw them to girls who watched his workouts – one almost fainted. "Leonard is like the Beatles," a publicist said. Then he knocked out Finch in three rounds and pocketed $1.5 million.

But when life imitates Hollywood – as Leonard's – it compels drama. In May Leonard was in Buffalo to fight another journeyman, Roger Stafford, when he experienced difficulty with his left eye. He was diagnosed with a partially detached retina and on May 15, 1982, underwent surgery at Johns Hopkins Hospital in Baltimore. Breathtakingly sudden, his future in boxing was uncertain, and Leonard stepped into the role of Hamlet.

CHAPTER 2

1982: Bait

LEONARD SUNK A HOOK – of the bait-and-tackle variety – into Hagler on the night of November 9, 1982. Whether it was the first hook is debatable, and certainly it wasn't the last, but it was sharp, intentionally cruel, and in the end it may have been the one that stuck deepest in Hagler's craw.

"A Night With Sugar Ray Leonard" was a press conference, a tribute, and a fund-raiser – a weird hybrid Leonard had arranged at Baltimore Civic Center to announce whether he would continue to be, or not to be, a boxer. That was the question, and it had hung over his head since his surgery for a detached retina on May 15.

Hagler, who flew in from his Massachusetts home, was there, as quarry and dupe. Cosell was there, as emcee, and Ali was there, as an unwitting example of what could become of Leonard if he quit too late. Entertainer Wayne Newton was in the house. Moreover, the public was invited, at $2 a head, with the proceeds pledged to summer jobs for Baltimore youth. Nobody could remember a public figure throwing open a press conference and charging admission.

Leonard had used its fund-raising mission as a reason to withhold his decision. The greater the suspense, the larger the crowd would be at the Civic Center, chosen because it had been the site of his pro debut in February 1977. More to the point, he craved the melodrama and attention, and so he artfully teased media and public in the weeks before the event. After Dr. Ronald Michels, the surgeon who repaired his eye, had declared it fit for the ring, Leonard was free to dangle both options.

Weeks earlier, Hagler, in Provincetown to prepare for an Oct. 30 bout, had been annoyed with Leonard's tease. "I'm tired of hearing Ray's name," said Hagler. "I'm getting to a point where I'm starting to really dislike this man. Because he's playing on the public, and the people can't see it."

Nonetheless, Leonard, as part of HBO's broadcasting team for Hagler's bout against Fulgencio Obelmejias in San Remo, Italy, kept it up. I was at San Remo for the *Boston Globe*, and buttonholed Leonard before the bout at Teatro Ariston.

"I can't wait for Nov. 9, if you get what I mean," he said. "Then I'll be done with this once and for all. I never said I was fighting Hagler, although some people thought I said something like that. Somebody said Marvin Hagler needs my help. He doesn't need my help. If anything, I would fight him because I wanted another title."

His comments were ambiguous, and later in the evening he was no clearer. After Hagler knocked out his opponent in the 5th round, Leonard interviewed him on air. "You don't want to quit until you come into Marvin's corner," Hagler said, amiably. They laughed about the money they could make – $15 million was projected for Leonard – at which point Leonard looked into the camera and said, "Mike, sign me up."

The next day the *Washington Post* picked up another of Leonard's remarks from a wire service: "His fight with Obel convinced me I am too light and too small to fight him." Four days later the *Post* caught up with him at the National Aquarium in Baltimore, where he had agreed to become the "honorary parent" of a stingray. "I have defeated so many monsters I feel like David and Goliath," Leonard said. "I killed all the giants but Marvelous Marvin. He would be a great triumph."

A bewildered sports media tried to stay abreast of the story, but each day seemed to bring a new and contradictory hint, dropped to a different reporter. "Leonard gives everyone good reason to believe whatever they want to believe," wrote Dave Kindred of the *Post*.

The public was kept guessing, as Leonard intended. On the evening of Nov. 9 an estimated 7,500 fans paid their way into the arena. Some paid $100 for "VIP" seats close to the ring.

Privately, Leonard was under pressure from his family – his wife and mother were insistent – and associates to retire. He was financially set, they argued, and boxing was too dangerous. Plenty of recent evidence supported their case.

Willie Classen, a 28-year-old journeyman middle-weight, had died on November 28, 1979, two days before Leonard's first title bout, a knockout victim of Wilford Scypion at Madison Square Garden. Three more fighters died in a three-week period preceding Leonard's wedding in January 1980, including a 13-year-old amateur in West Virginia who had fought three matches in a single day without headgear.

Then, in June 1980, as fans filed into Montreal's Olympic Stadium for the first Leonard-Duran match, two Canadian lightweights squared off in a preliminary bout. Leonard, who was in his dressing room, did not see the match between Cleveland Denny and Gaetan Hart. This was their third meeting, each having beaten the other once. Through nine rounds and two minutes of the final round their rivalry remained virtually on even terms. In the final minute, inexplicably and without warning, Denny wilted. For about 20 seconds Denny absorbed a powerful and incessant pounding – film would show him taking 12 hard punches to the head in a seven-second span. Hart later described the final blows as "a right that made his eyes roll followed by a left hook." The referee, later criticized for waiting too long, stopped the bout with 12 seconds remaining as Denny slumped to the canvas, unconscious.

"Hart's fists had driven Denny's tongue down his throat and ruptured blood vessels in his head," a Montreal sportswriter wrote.

Denny, a 24-year-old native of Guyana, died 17 days later, leaving a wife and infant son. Except for its high visibility, Denny's death was grimly typical. Since the end of World War II the sport had averaged 12.4 deaths per year. Most resulted from the short-term effects of cerebral hemorrhage on the surface of the brain, known as subdural hematoma. In such deaths swelling and impaired blood flow deprived the brain of oxygen, compressed the brain stem, and caused unconsciousness and coma. Beyond the deaths were countless numbers of punch-drunk former boxers who suffered from memory loss, speech impairment, unsteady gait, tremors, and episodes of confusion and depression. Former heavyweight champion Joe Louis had been a textbook case, until his death in 1981, and now Ali was on his way toward becoming one.

Another high-profile death occurred on November 5, 1980, 20 days before the Leonard-Duran rematch. Bantamweight Johnny Owen of England, knocked out by champion Lupe Pintor in a September 19 title bout, succumbed in a Los Angeles hospital. Owen, British journalist Hugh McIlvanney wrote, was a desperately shy 24-year-old who had never kissed a girl and had found his only means of expression in a boxing ring. "It is his tragedy that he found himself articulate in such a dangerous language," wrote McIlvanney.

Five deaths occurred in 1982 before Leonard's November press conference, while another fighter, a Nigerian featherweight named Young Ali, lay in a coma after being knocked out by Barry McGuigan in England, soon to succumb. The British Medical Association called for boxing to be outlawed in England, where the sport was spawned in the 18th century.

These ghosts, then, provided a Greek chorus to Leonard's unfolding drama. Voices from the living were heard, too. Harold Weston Jr., a former welterweight contender, had suffered a detached retina in a 1979 bout. Though it had been surgically repaired, Weston was unable to obtain a license to fight in New York because his surgeon had told officials boxing posed "considerable risk" to his eyesight. Weston retired and became assistant matchmaker at Madison Square Garden. "I want this in big bold letters – I advise Ray Leonard not to fight anymore," Weston said after Leonard's surgery. "If he don't quit I'll go up there and beat him with a stick."

"An Evening With Sugar Ray Leonard," a columnist wrote, was rather like Leonard's fights – a slow start that built toward a heroic finish. A highlight film was shown, as Cosell provided commentary and the crowd cheered Leonard's victories over Wilfredo Benitez, Roberto Duran, Ayub Kalule, and Hearns. Ali, in words slurred but mirthful, talked about the traits he shared with Leonard – shuffling, dancing, and good looks. "Boxers have been known to be ugly but we are pretty," Ali said, patting Leonard on his smooth unmarked cheeks." He suggested that if Leonard returned to the ring he "might become the greatest ever."

Hagler's introduction was politely applauded. The tuxedo-clad middleweight champion, shaved skull burnished, climbed through the ropes, hugged Leonard, and took the microphone. Earlier Leonard had struggled to hold back tears, but now he was still and watchful. Hagler's comments verged from awkward to tone-deaf.

He cautioned Leonard against ending up like Joe Louis, and added, "Ali, sorry." Leonard appeared oblivious to Hagler's faux pas, so intent was his concentration. After Hagler others spoke, including Wayne Newton, who told a tepid joke about being part Native American.

At last it was Leonard's turn. His post-surgery role as Hamlet had come to its climax. He played it with conviction, as he gestured and moved about the ring, paced his delivery, made eye contact with his invited guests and audience, and built suspense. He talked of beauty, and how, in his eyes, everyone important to him was beautiful.

"Very few people get a second chance to visualize how beautiful the world really is," Leonard said. "I had the blessing to be able to see again."

Beauty is a parent, a son, an advisor, an attorney, a manager, and a trainer, he said. All were present – Cicero and Getha Leonard, Ray Jr., Janks Morton, Mike Trainer, Ollie Dunlap, Angelo Dundee – and all were beautiful as seen through his restored vision. He looked at his wife, Juanita, seated at ringside.

"Beauty is a woman, a woman who deals with criticism society has made, and stands behind you no matter what."

Slowly, Leonard drifted toward the corner closest to where Hagler was seated.

"In one second I'll tell you what I will do."

The audience held its breath. Leonard gazed upon Hagler, whose tongue flicked across his lower lip as his rugged face tilted upward.

"A fight with this great man, this great champion,

would be one of the greatest fights in the history of boxing."

Applause. He was going to do it.

"Talk about money; talkin' Fort Knox."

More applause. Cheers.

He was at the ropes now, a finger pointed at Hagler.

"And this is the only man who can make that possible – Marvelous Marvin Hagler."

The fight of the century!

"But unfortunately, it'll never happen."

Huh?

"Thank you and God bless you all."

There was a moment of confusion. Had Leonard meant he would not fight at all, or not fight Hagler? The question was shouted from outside the ring.

"No, that's it, that's it," Leonard said.

Historian and journalist Bert Sugar recalled how, at that instant, Hagler's face fell. "He had sat there all night, smiling," Sugar recalled. "And all of sudden, like those two Grecian figures of comedy and drama, it dropped."

Another journalist in attendance, Steve Farhood, recalled thinking that Leonard had humiliated Hagler.

"Here's Marvin sitting like an obedient dog and he gets shunted aside," Farhood said.

Hagler moved toward the nearest exit. "I think he'll fight again," Hagler told a TV reporter.

If the audience and Hagler had been caught by surprise, Leonard's confidantes were not. They knew he had given *Sports Illustrated* his decision a week earlier, and that the story would hit the stands the next day.

Nearly 20 years later, Leonard reflected on his exquisite tease of Hagler.

"Was it cold to have him there, knowing full well that I was going to say no," Leonard said, in an interview with ESPN. "Yeah, it was pretty cold. But was it smart to have him there? Yes, it was smart to have him there, because that was kind of the start of this whole Hagler-Leonard thing that made it what it was in '87."

At the time, Leonard recalled, he had not known for certain he would fight Hagler. But he must have had a premonition, based on his response when asked if the invitation to Hagler had been a "taunt."

"A little bit – a little bit," Leonard said. "I just wanted to create that drama, that intrigue. I did that."

CHAPTER 3

· · · · · · · · · · · · · · · · · · · ·

1973: Million Dollar Smile

THEY FIRST INTERSECTED IN the old mill town of Lowell, Mass., at the national Golden Gloves tournament, in March 1973. Neither laid a glove on the other, with Leonard at 132 pounds, and Hagler at 156. Still, their alchemy of opposites was sparked, and their tale set in motion.

Leonard was noticed for his smile, a dazzling beam of wholesome seduction. A reporter for the *Lowell Sun* wrote:

> Ray Leonard's million dollar smile has helped carry him into the 132-pound National Golden Gloves championship final tonight.
>
> The Washington DC boxer will square off against Hilmer Kenty of Columbus, and if his teeth are in good working order it could be a cakewalk for Mr. Leonard.
>
> "My mouth is my main weapon," proclaimed the 16-year-old Parkdale High stu-

dent. "I psych my opponents out by smiling at them. They don't know what to make of it."

Leonard has grinned his way to an impressive 35-2 record including one KO and 3 decisions in the current National Tournament.

Leonard beat Kenty in a decision for his first major national title.

On the same page the *Lowell Sun* ran another story, about Hagler after his loss in the 156-pound semifinal to Dale Grant of Salt Lake City. Earlier in the tournament, reporter Rick Harrison had coined the moniker "Marvelous Marvin" in print. Now Harrison described Hagler, 18, alone in the locker room, as he dressed slowly and dejectedly.

One could hardly blame Hagler if he didn't want to talk to anyone at all. But that isn't Marvin's style, as he discussed the bitter setback openly.

"I wanted that national title too bad. I wanted to win so much I think I tried too hard," stated the Brockton resident.

Hagler went on to say that he could have beaten Grant with "a little more time" and that next year he would "be back." But his optimism did not override the sense of gloom and frustration. For the first time, the adjective "bitter" and Hagler were joined in print.

Leonard and Hagler did not speak to one another,

though they likely caught one another's eye. Hagler had defeated one of Leonard's teammates in an early round, and later, in the locker room, had consoled the tearful young man. The *Lowell Sun* articles had run on the same page. If either boxer had read the story about himself, he could not have missed the other. Hagler almost certainly would have made note of Leonard winning the 132-pound title.

Ollie Dunlap, Leonard's longtime administrator, believes Hagler had his eyes on Leonard from the start of the tournament.

"This was Marvin's home turf but Ray was getting all the pub – all the reporters migrated over to Ray in the gym – and it really bothered Marvin," Dunlap said.

Leonard was 16, and already a wily rascal. Indeed, just the summer before, he had fibbed about his age and affiliation in two failed attempts to make the 1972 Olympic team.

More than most his age, he knew who he was and where he was going. He was a celebrity at Parkdale High. He was the fifth child of Cicero and Getha Leonard, who owned a one-story ranch on Barlowe Road in Palmer Park, Md., just outside Washington, D.C. He was the boyfriend of Juanita Wilkinson, the cute 15-year-old who lived five blocks away and was pregnant.

He was the boxer who smiled in the ring. Until, that is, he took aim at his opponent's head. Out of the ring he affected a similar duality. He was polite and good-natured, unless he was crossed or doubted – then he was cold, judgmental and abrupt. Once, returning from an out-of-state tournament, he was told another boy had been telephoning Juanita. He cornered the boy at the recreation center, next to the jukebox, snapped off a left hook, and opened a seven-stitch gash. The center's director, Ollie Dunlap, suspended him for a month.

He was considerate of his teammates at the Palmer Park Recreation Center. He even offered to cash in an airplane ticket – provided by officials eager to have him box in an amateur tournament – and rent a van so that all of his teammates could travel. He was egotistical enough to refuse to display his membership card at the entrance. "Everybody knows who I am," he announced.

He was fascinated with imagery and media, quick to grasp that grooming, clothing, manners, and speech projected an image, and that image was a powerful force. Boxing gave him entry into a world of travel, hotels, restaurants, and private clubs that was unknown to his family. "What are the different forks for?" he asked at his first upscale restaurant. He learned to use the appropriate fork, just as he learned to be meticulous about his clothing. He carried a small dictionary to help with vocabulary, and took tap dance lessons to learn graceful movement. Imagery was as vital to Leonard as any punch he could throw or duck. Media, the conduit of images, infatuated him as much as boxing.

From his mother, Getha, came determination and ambition to improve himself. Getha was an affectionate woman, but also high-strung and opinionated, known to enjoy an argument and a drink. She would have smothered Leonard if he had not decided, at an early age, to keep her at bay.

From his father, Cicero, came the macho and will to

dominate. Cicero was quiet, uncomplaining, and plain talking. He taught Leonard by example more than by hands-on parenting.

Both parents handed down a blue-collar ethic that served him in the gym. Both were skilled chefs whose savory southern basics fueled Leonard's appetite for life.

Leonard owed much to his high-spirited brother, Roger, who was three years older, the third son, after Roy and Kenny. As an 8-year-old, Leonard followed Roger to a gym in Washington, D.C., for his first taste of boxing. Though he didn't like it, neither did he like being teased and swatted around by Roger. This became his impetus to learn self-defense. A few years later, as new residents of Palmer Park, Roger pestered the recreation center to start a boxing program, and this time Leonard found it more to his liking. Subsequently, it was Roger who sacrificed his nose – several times – to the swift merciless blows of his younger brother.

He was born Ray Charles Leonard, on May 17, 1956, in Wilmington, N.C. Getha named him for the legendary R&B musician who later would sing "America the Beautiful" before one of his biggest fights. As a child Leonard sang sweetly in a church choir, and Getha likened him to Sam Cooke, another R&B star. But Leonard dropped out of the choir when he started boxing, which was just as well. His post-pubescent voice became the butt of family jokes. "Ray went from singin' to swingin'," the Leonards would chuckle.

Cicero and Getha grew up and met in South Carolina. Cicero's father, Bidge, a sharecropper, was a towering thick-chested man, who according to family lore once knocked out a mule to win a $10 bet. Cicero boxed as a youth, inspired by his hero, heavyweight champion Joe Louis. On the farm his father rented, he set up a ring with iron spikes and plough lines and invited neighbors over to box. When he came of age, Cicero left the farm and joined the Navy. During World War II Cicero boxed for the Navy team, as a stocky 150-pounder, and claimed to have won all but one of 70 bouts.

After the war Cicero and Getha married and started their family in Wilmington, N.C., a city whose history included an infamous 1898 riot in which scores of blacks were killed and progressives – black and white – were banished by rampaging white supremacists. The riot suppressed black political participation in North Carolina and explained why the civil rights movement lagged there in the 1950s and 1960s. Cicero worked on an assembly line at a Coca-Cola bottling plant, but in 1960 he and Getha moved to Washington, D.C., in search of better jobs. Leonard was four when he left Wilmington, too young to remember much about it.

The Leonards rented an apartment at L Street and New Jersey in the District. Cicero loaded trucks in a produce market and Getha worked as a nursing assistant. The cramped apartment now included their two youngest daughters, Sandy and Sharonette, whose care often fell to the oldest daughter, Linda.

Leonard grew into a shy, quiet child who stayed out of trouble and usually spoke only if spoken to. Protected from schoolyard bullies by Roger, he expended his considerable energy playing basketball, tumbling, and running.

© Ollie Dunlap

Father Cicero Leonard, left,
Sugar Ray Leonard, and
mother Getha Leonard, right.

At home he liked to curl up on the floor and read comic books. Superman was his favorite.

To Cicero and Getha, the American Dream started with home ownership and a lawn. By 1967 they had saved enough for a down payment on a house in Seat Pleasant, Md., a community east of the District. The next year they moved to Palmer Park, an unincorporated township of 9,000 mostly black working-class residents just across the District's northeast line. Their one-story ranch was small, to be sure, and the mortgage payments left little in their budget. But it had back and front yards, room enough for 12-year-old Ray to play with his dog "King," and to entertain neighbors with cartwheels and flips.

Less happy was Roger, who missed his old boxing club in the District. His love of boxing propelled him to the new Palmer Park Recreation Center virtually across the street. The county-funded center had a mission of keeping Palmer Park youth off the streets, and particularly out of nearby Landover Mall, which had become a vipers-nest of drugs, guns, and prostitution. Ever assertive, Roger asked the center's director, Ollie Dunlap, to start a boxing program.

Dunlap, 29, was just a year removed from the Washington Redskins taxi squad as a 212-pound linebacker during

Vince Lombardi's single season as coach and GM. It was Lombardi's wife, Marie, who had helped him land the job as director of the community center. The son of a career military man, Dunlap's thin knowledge of boxing had come from watching the Friday night fights on TV with his father in the 1950s. Dunlap considered Roger's request.

For much of America boxing was an anachronism in 1970. Body bags returned from Vietnam, while Muhammad Ali, stripped of his heavyweight title for refusing his 1967 induction, remained a symbol of the war's divisiveness. Without Ali, boxing lacked a marquee star. The numbers of gyms, amateur clubs, and professional shows had been in decline since the 1930s. America's white middle class was indifferent to a sport dominated by black and Latino fighters, and leaned toward a view of boxing as primitive and brutal. The absence of college athletic scholarships for boxers further undercut its appeal. The NCAA had dropped boxing in 1960 after a boxer died of a brain injury suffered in the 1959 national tourney.

But the Big Picture did not deter Dunlap, who valued self-discipline and ran the recreation center with old-school authority. He knew boxing demanded the self-discipline his young clients needed, and he figured if boxing could lure a few from the mall it was worth a try. A bulletin board request for volunteer coaches brought forth three – Dave Jacobs, Janks Morton, and Joe "Pepe" Saunders, who later became known as Pepe Correa.

Among the first to sign up were Roger, of course, and Derrik Holmes, a gregarious 14-year-old who was Ray's best friend. Prodded by his brother and Holmes, Leon-

© Ollie Dunlap

Trainer Dave Jacobs, left, taught young Ray Leonard sound fundamentals at the Palmer Park Recreation Center.

ard signed up, too. Saunders gave him his first boxing lesson, but Jacobs quickly became his coach. A former amateur champion from the District, the 37-year-old Jacobs had boxed briefly as a pro, and now drove a delivery van for a pharmacy to support his wife and six children.

Jacobs stressed hard work, moral fiber, and as a technical matter, balance. The latter was crucial to avoid going down on the hardwood basketball court that doubled as a boxing ring. The rec center had no money to buy an actual ring, so Dunlap laid tape on the court.

At a bony 100 pounds, Leonard looked at risk of being toppled by a strong breeze. Yet, he quickly established himself as educable, eager and determined. In the mornings, before school, he showed up for roadwork, and after school he dependably made it to the gym. A few weeks of instruction revealed his gifts to Jacobs. He had the deluxe package: speed, power, stamina, guile, and instinct. Gradually, his success in the ring would transform his introverted personality. His shyness would melt away as he learned to talk with his gloves.

In the next year Leonard added 25 pounds and breezed through local novice competition, earning his first men-

© Ollie Dunlap

Sugar Ray Leonard and his first trainer, Dave Jacobs.

tion in the *Washington Post* on August 10, 1971. Robert Herzog wrote that he "unveiled a devastating left hand that swelled and bloodied the eye of his opponent, Leroy Carlton. The culmination of this bloodbath came at 1:51 of the 3rd round on a left-right combination by Leonard that put Carlton on the canvas for good."

Leonard threw a left hook so violent that if it missed his momentum often would pitch him onto the canvas, according to one of his first coaches, Pepe Correa. If it connected he inquired about his opponent's health.

"He'd hit you in the chin with a left hook and he'd ask, 'are you okay?'" said Correa. "And if you said yes? You got hit with the same hook. Deep inside, you knew that he could really hurt you and really wanted to hurt you."

Soon Leonard was matched with Bobby Magruder, a 132-pounder out of the nearby Hillcrest Boys and Girls Club who was touted as the best amateur in the District area. Leonard and Magruder fought three "wars," with Leonard the victor in each. Local fans so hotly antici-

© Ollie Dunlap

At 15, Sugar Ray Leonard boxed for Palmer Park
Recreation Center. (l–r) trainer Dave Jacobs, Ray Leonard,
Derrik Holmes, Brayson Mason, Roger Leonard.

pated their third meeting that it was moved from Hillcrest to the larger Prince George's Community College.

Cicero now worked long hours as night manager of a supermarket just across the District line. Though Cicero initially had been skeptical of his youngest son's ring ability, he had become his biggest booster. Leonard returned the affection, sometimes showing up at the supermarket at midnight to help his father stock shelves. He would return home by 2:30 a.m., sleep for three hours, and arise for the morning roadwork demanded by Jacobs. After school Leonard would be at the gym for bag work and sparring, as well as basketball, which he loved to play. By dinner he was tired, and he routinely slumbered in the evening when he should have been doing homework. Finally, Dunlap laid down the law: rec center privileges would require a 'C' average. Those with 'B' and 'A' averages would get more time in the center's basketball games. Leonard got the message and improved his grades.

1973: The Sugar in Ray

By the spring of 1972 Leonard had the attention of amateur boxing officials as they looked ahead to the Summer Olympics at Munich. He was hard to miss. For one thing, he mimicked Muhammad Ali's signature "shuffle" – a blur-like oscillation of feet while in an elevated posture. For another, he threw Kid Gavilan's "bolo" punch – an upward punch delivered from the hip in the traditional manner that Filipinos throw a bolo knife.

The shuffle and bolo were designed for theatricality, and usually got a rise out of the crowd. They had the added effect of distracting Leonard's opponents and luring them into mistakes.

Jacobs pushed Leonard into elite competition, and though he lost in the quarterfinals of the national AAU tournament, he impressed the assistant coach of the U.S. boxing team, Sarge Johnson. It was Johnson who included Leonard on an American team that boxed against several European teams before the Olympic trials.

One day Johnson watched Leonard work out, and whispered in Jacobs' ear, "That kid of yours is sweeter than sugar." The comparison to the legendary Sugar Ray Robinson, in hand and foot speed, and in graceful and stylish movement, was high praise. Indeed, Leonard evoked Robinson, the former welterweight and middleweight champion whose heyday was the 1940s and early 1950s. The nickname stuck and Sugar Ray Leonard was born.

The birth of Sugar Ray Leonard gave shape and form

to the alter ego with the seductive smile, smooth patter, and sly intent – though not for another ten years would it reach full maturity. Nearly thirty years later Leonard's ex-wife would reflect upon his slick alter ego. "If you knew Ray Leonard prior to him becoming Sugar Ray Leonard, you would see two totally different people," Juanita Leonard said. "Ray Leonard was a very quiet, meek, giving, caring individual. A peacemaker. A very loving individual – a very, very caring and giving individual. Sugar Ray Leonard, on the other hand, is probably the total opposite of that."

Leonard quickly began to explore his Sugar Ray persona. Determined to make the U.S. Olympic team, he ran up against a seemingly insurmountable obstacle. The amateur governing body required that fighters be at least 17 to qualify for the Olympics, but Leonard had only turned 16 in May. He and Jacobs came up with a plan: they would lie.

The top AAU boxing official, Rollie Schwartz, recalled meeting Leonard at an international meet against a Soviet team prior to the Olympic trials. The AAU had an age requirement of 17 for international competition.

"I looked at the choir boy face of this kid and I had a sneaking suspicion he wasn't quite that old," Schwartz said. "I asked him how old he was and he said, 'I'm seventeen, sir,' without batting an eye."

Officials allowed Leonard to compete, and in the 1st round he knocked out his Russian opponent, who was 22 or 23 and more experienced. The meet, held in Las Vegas, provided Leonard his first brush with celebrity

– comic Redd Foxx, former heavyweight champion Joe Louis – and neon. He was dazzled and smitten.

After his strong showing in Las Vegas he was favored to win the Olympic trials in Cincinnati. But he lost a disputed decision in the semifinal to a local fighter, Greg Whaley. This loss should have ended Leonard's 1972 Olympic quest, except that now, as Sugar Ray, it didn't. If Leonard could dissemble about his age he could do so about his affiliation.

Under a special exemption, boxers in the military advanced automatically to the Olympic box-off. Jacobs, with the tacit approval of other amateur officials, arranged for Leonard to be a "member" of the Army team. But this ruse also failed. The night before his bout Leonard and a teammate devoured a cake. The feast pushed Leonard above 125 pounds, and in an effort to run off the excess weight he became dehydrated and ill. A physician scratched him from the tournament.

Juanita Wilkinson became Leonard's girlfriend around this time. She was a small, pretty, serious-minded 14-year-old, one of five daughters raised by a single father, Dick Wilkinson, who managed a gas station. The Wilkinsons lived five blocks from the Leonards, and from Dick Wilkinson's front porch Landover Mall was visible. In the summer and fall of 1972 Leonard and Juanita often were on the front porch when Dick Wilkinson came home from work, and he didn't know whether to be glad his daughter was not at the mall, or worried that Leonard's smile was too angelic. Juanita took to attending Leonard's workouts at the rec center, and at local tournaments she usually was in the crowd, though she found boxing distasteful.

"He was a scrawny little fellow with a really big Afro, and not an appealing (looking) person," Juanita recalled. "But there was just something about him, and he was different. He was very shy, very to himself...that was the thing that caught my eye about him, as opposed to his looks."

Characteristic of Leonard was his knack for turning defeat and adversity into motivation, a trait he may have internalized from one of his screen heroes, Bruce Lee, the martial arts icon, whose catlike moves and evasions could be seen in Leonard's ring maneuvers. After missing out on the 1972 Olympics, he found a girlfriend and shifted his focus to the next Olympics, four years distant. When Leonard ventured to Massachusetts in March of 1973 his eyes were on Montreal for the 1976 Summer Games.

CHAPTER 4

. . . .

1973: Fathered by Adversity

MARVIN HAGLER CARRIED HIS portable TV into the Sheraton Boston, the hotel for the New England amateur boxing team, in May 1973. Another "major," the national AAU tournament, was about to begin. His trainer, Goody Petronelli, asked him why the TV set.

"Because I plan to stay the week," Hagler said.

Indeed, both Hagler and Leonard, who was on the Washington, D.C., team, stayed the week and advanced to the finals.

The *Boston's Globe*'s Bob Ryan wrote:

> Picking the Best Performer at last night's AAU Boxing Tournament at the Hynes Auditorium was about as easy as naming Frank Sinatra's greatest hit.
>
> Was it flashy Ray Leonard, the 139-pound whiz from Washington, D.C., who evoked

comparisons with Sugar Ray Robinson, Willie Pep and Muhammad Ali in punching out a dazzling decision over tough Pete Ranzany?

...Or was it local favorite Marvin Hagler, the newest Brockton belter, who flattened Philadelphian Melvin Hackett with a gorgeous right hook to move into tonight's finals?

...As awesome as the powerful victories by (Mike) Hess and Hagler were, the performance which impressed many observers most was that of Leonard, the 17-year-old machine from D.C. This kid is sophisticated enough to throw a left hook off a left jab, and he again delighted the buffs with a great boxing show.

Before the final Hagler made it known he was turning pro after the tournament – a decision he had come to only since the Golden Gloves.

The decision to turn pro, rather than wait for the '76 Olympics, as did Leonard, defined Hagler as much as any single decision. It prolonged his rise through the ranks and cost him millions in exposure and marketability. But the reasons for it were plain. Hagler was two years older than Leonard and no longer in school. Preparing for the Olympics would have pulled Hagler away from his day job in construction at a time when he needed more money, not less. He did not have the "luxury" of two working parents who owned a home, as had Leonard.

Indeed, the absence of a father is a gap in Hagler's biography that he chose to leave blank. Hagler never spoke of his father publicly, though unspoken was the presumption that no child is unscarred by parental abandonment. In Hagler the scar carved out a deeply distrustful nature.

Both Goody and Pat Petronelli were told by Hagler that his father was in a New Jersey state prison. Oblique reference was made to a murder conviction. But they never were provided details, or corroboration, and they never were sure if it was so.

In 1982 an 18-year-old man showed up in Brockton claiming to be Hagler's half-brother. The man claimed Hagler's father had had an affair with his mother. Hagler put the man up in a hotel and checked out his story. It proved to be bogus, and Hagler put the would-be scam artist back out on the street. But the incident suggested that Hagler's father, wherever he was, had not been imprisoned eighteen years prior, if ever.

Hagler's lineage provided him magnificent boxing genes – that much was certain. He was graced with long arms and shoulders as wide as his ambition. More remarkable was his temporalis – a muscle that runs across the skull at both temples. Most temporalis muscles are a quarter-inch thick, but both of Hagler's were one inch, a phenomenon that astounded his physician when it was discovered during a routine exam in 1983. Hagler's temporalis acted as a natural helmet and almost certainly helped him absorb blows. But he was sensitive to the notion of freakish physicality, perhaps from a racial perspective, and bridled at questions about his temporalis.

Before he was Marvelous Marvin he was Marvin Nathaniel Hagler, born on May 23, 1954, in Newark. Early in his career his age was a matter of uncertainty, some believing he was born in 1953 or 1952. Most of the articles about Hagler in the 1970s made him a year or two older than he later claimed to be. Hagler was complicit in the continuing inaccuracy because, he believed, it generated talk and publicity. When he legally changed his name to "Marvelous Marvin" in 1982, he produced a birth certificate that settled the matter.

Hagler's mother, Ida Mae, was one of two daughters born to Bessie and Luther Hagler in Logan, West Virginia. The Haglers moved to Newark in 1941. There, Bessie and Luther divorced and Bessie married James Monroe. Ida Mae's half-brothers, James and Eugene Monroe, were born before Bessie took her children to Fayetteville, N.C., where Bessie worked in a US Army kitchen at Fort Bragg.

In 1947 Bessie and James Monroe moved their brood back to Newark and opened a small restaurant on Boyd Street. They served up soul food and made a modest living. Ida Mae, who called herself "Mae," and her sister, Amy, known as "Tiny," rushed back from school to wait on customers at lunch hour, and after school they helped clean up. Years later Mae recalled polishing stools and "hating" it.

At 15, Mae met Robert Sims, a classmate who was a singer in a local "doo-wop" band. Sims, tall and wiry, had grown up in Newark, the son of a foundry worker. After Mae met Sims she gave birth to Marvin, just short of her 17th birthday. Mae never identified Sims as Marvin's father, and later, when Marvin's younger brother Robbie Sims fought as a pro, he was identified as Hagler's half-brother. Mae's second child, Veronica (Ronnie), was born a year after Marvin.

Mae and Robert Sims married in April 1956. He took a job as a warehouseman at a pickle factory. When Bessie's restaurant fell victim to urban renewal, Mae found work as a housekeeper. Over the next eight years Mae gave birth to Sherry, Robert Jr. (Robbie), Gennara, and Noreen. Sims also fathered another daughter, Sharon, who was raised by Mae.

After the birth of Noreen, in 1964, Sims left Mae. She and the children lived in a tenement apartment in the crumbling central ward and barely scraped by. One evening, her landlord pounded on the door and harangued her for the rent. Ten-year-old Marvin witnessed the scene with humiliation and anger, and vowed to buy her a house. Despite working as a housekeeper for a South Orange, N.J., family, and doing in-home catering on Jewish holidays, Mae never had enough money at the end of the month. She went on welfare for more than a year.

While Mae worked two jobs, Marvin and Veronica tended the household. He kept the apartment clean, and she scrubbed and dressed the younger children. The family was warm and loving, and Mae often told her children, "As long as I've got you I'm a rich woman."

"A lot of days I only had time to change from one uniform to another," Mae recalled. "I was tired, but the kids could be so funny and make me laugh. It made me feel so good."

Marvin made his way on the streets and playgrounds as a better-than-average baseball, football, and basketball player. He was nicknamed "Short Stuff" and occasionally was required to defend himself against an assortment of toughs. Mae insisted. "I hit you with a stick, brick and bottle – anything I could get my hands on," Hagler recalled. "And kicked you when you were down. It was known as survival. My mother taught me, 'You better not come back crying.'"

If Hagler needed inspiration, a poster of former heavyweight champion Floyd Patterson hung on a nearby telephone pole. Hagler removed the poster, tacked it to his bedroom wall, and told his mother that he meant to have his face on a poster. He was given a pair of beat-up boxing gloves, which he used mostly for fun.

But there was another side to the young Hagler, withdrawn, brooding, artistic. He spent hours drawing finely detailed cartoons that delighted his siblings and garnered encouragement from his mother. When he craved solitude, which was often, Hagler climbed to the rooftop of his tenement. There, in a few crates, he tended to wounded pigeons, in whose potential for flight he seemed to draw comfort, just as would future heavyweight champion Mike Tyson on the rooftops of Bedford-Stuyvesant. On the stairwell at the rear of his apartment young Marvin kept a pet turtle. One day Mae came home horrified to find the turtle in the bathtub. When she ordered Marvin to remove it, he protested, "Ma, that's the only place he's got to swim."

In July 1967, when Hagler was 13, Newark's ghetto

rioted. Newark's ghetto was not the first to riot in the 1960s, or the last. But it was typical, in that its black residents were fed up with racist police and city officials, crumbling schools and services, and menial low-paying jobs. Whites, though now a minority in Newark, were the cops, firefighters, teachers, store managers, bank tellers, clerks, and landlords. Hagler brushed up against them on a daily basis, but for all intents and purposes they lived across a profound divide. His childhood mistrust of whites was formed in this toxic climate of de facto segregation.

Initially Hagler watched the riot from the window of his tenement. He watched the looting of stores, torching of vehicles, and the rage of people long exploited and victimized. From above, the looters looked like ants toting crumbs on a picnic table, he thought, struggling under couches and appliances.

He watched the virtually all-white Newark Police and State Police and National Guard try to subdue the rioters, who were almost all black. Inevitably a bullet caromed off the side of the tenement, at which time Mae ordered everybody to get below window level. Mae grabbed 3-year-old Noreen and dropped to the floor. One by one, all of Mae's children huddled on the floor.

"Until I say so, nobody stands up," Mae said.

For three days nobody stood up. They crawled on their bellies, like soldiers in combat. They slid on pillows. They slept underneath their beds. Sirens wailed as they watched television news detailing the carnage – Newark was in flames. When the riot stopped 23 people lay dead, 725 people were injured and close to 1500 people had been arrested.

Finally, it was okay to stand up.

"This is no place to live," said Mae.

Two years later, in May 1969, Newark's ghetto erupted again, after the shooting death of a black 17-year-old boy by a black cop. The shooting unnerved Mae – Marvin was now 15 and prime fodder for the streets. Urged by relatives, Mae moved her family to Brockton, Massachusetts, in 1970. The fact that Brockton was the hometown of former heavyweight champion Rocky Marciano meant nothing to Mae. She just wanted to live where it was peaceful.

Brockton had one-sixth the population of Newark, and little of the racial volatility, but in its own way was just as gritty. A crusty old mill town, and once a shoe-manufacturing center, Brockton was frayed at the edges, the shoe and leather industry largely departed. The high school was one of the largest on the east coast, with a strong athletic tradition, especially in football. Its teams were nicknamed the Boxers – just one reminder that Marciano's spirit hovered over the city.

Mae rented an apartment on the less affluent east side. Soon she found catering and housekeeping work, while Marvin, who had quit high school in Newark, found a $2-an-hour job in a tannery.

Two pivotal events ensued. First came Hagler's 98-pound weakling moment, not in the classic manner of sand kicked in his face, but from the fists of a Brockton tough, Donnell Wigfall, an amateur boxer. The slightly chubby 16-year-old took a beating in a fight, supposedly after a party, over a girl.

In 1971 Hagler climbed the stairs to the Petronelli School of Boxing, above a hardware store, in downtown Brockton. He came in quietly, found a seat, watched the boxers train, and left just as quietly. The next day he was back, and the next. After a few days, co-owner Guerino Petronelli, known as Goody, noticed the intent and curious youth.

"You want to learn how to box?" Petronelli asked.

"Yeah."

"Why is that?"

"I want to be a champion."

So began the boxing career of Hagler, in a manner not unlike thousands of other boxers before and after.

Goody and Pat Petronelli (49 and 51 years old, respectively) were in their third year of operation, hoping to strike gold but realistic enough to continue to run their construction company. In 1969 their childhood buddy, Marciano, the retired former heavyweight champion, was ready to partner in the gym. Then a small aircraft carrying Marciano went down in Iowa. Brockton lost its most famous citizen, and the Petronellis lost a friend and backer. The Petronelli brothers, sons of Italian immigrants, tacked up photos of Marciano and opened the gym anyway. Goody, a pro boxer prior to a 25-year-plus Navy hitch during which he coached boxing, became head trainer. Pat, who boxed as an amateur and managed Goody's pro career, ran the gym and helped out with the boxers.

Goody and Pat represented the yin and yang of boxing. Goody was literal and unemotional, while Pat was intuitive and sensitive. Goody talked to a fighter about the angle and leverage of a jab. Pat talked to the same fighter about his girlfriend or family problems. Their styles were complementary, built to nurture a moody virtuoso, but Hagler had no way of knowing this when he arrived in 1971. Newark's de facto segregation had made him leery of whites.

In those first weeks the Petronellis found out how much Hagler wanted to be a boxer. Goody worked with him in the ring, watched him get punched by more advanced kids, and worked with him some more. After awhile Goody noticed that Hagler was learning faster than the others.

One evening Goody said, "Marvin, you're picking it up pretty good."

"I been practicin', man."

"How have you been practicing?"

"I been practicin' in the mirror at home."

On most evenings, Hagler was first to arrive and last to leave. One evening as he sparred he was gashed above an eye. The brothers knew young fighters were spooked by blood and half-expected Hagler to quit. But the next evening he returned to pound the bags and jump rope.

"This kid is different," Goody told his brother.

Hagler's determination was fueled by the birth of his first child in Newark. Hagler never publicly acknowledged the mother of the boy, Gentry, who sometimes was called "Monk." This was also the period he resumed a friendship with 18-year-old Bertha Washington, a small, pretty, saucer-eyed girl whom he had known since childhood.

Bertha, one of ten children raised in an east Brockton public housing project, had given birth to her first child, Jimmy, in 1970. She would have a daughter, Celeste, in 1972, before taking up with Hagler.

When Hagler fought his first amateur bout, in South Boston, the Petronellis introduced him to photographer Angie Carlino as "Short Stuff Hagler," not convinced that "Marvin" was a proper ring name. By 1973 Hagler was the top amateur in their stable, and "Short Stuff" had been dropped.

Now he was 156 pounds of lean, chiseled muscle, a byproduct of working for Petronelli Construction, which specialized in masonry. Each morning he pulled on a work shirt and steel-toed boots and went off to haul brick and push wheelbarrows of cement for $4 an hour. The money never stretched far enough, with a son in Newark and his mother and siblings needing help.

The Petronellis noticed that Hagler occasionally skipped lunch. Other times he pulled out a dollar and bought a sandwich. Most of his paycheck, they realized, was going to his mother. They worried, because a construction worker who boxes must eat, as must a boxer who works construction. One day the Petronellis invited Hagler out to lunch. He ordered his usual sandwich, and when the bill came he pulled out his dollar.

"Put it away," said Pat Petronelli.

Hagler assumed the lunch money would be subtracted from his paycheck. At the end of the week he opened his pay envelope to a pleasant surprise. Lunch was free, although Hagler was sure no such thing existed.

Weeks and months passed and the Petronellis picked up more lunches, repaid only in Hagler's gratitude. His suspicion of white people, rooted in the racial acrimony of Newark, no longer applied to Goody and Pat Petronelli. They did not pry into his personal life, but as his trust increased he opened up to them. Later, when his career stalled, Hagler would be pressured to leave the Petronellis, but he never did. They were his surrogate fathers.

Their relationship was such that, by the time Hagler fought Leonard, they worked without a contract. When the Petronellis asked for one to formalize their one-third share, which figured to be no less than $4 million (and turned out to be more than $6 million), Hagler was offended.

"Marv looked at us and said, 'After all these years you want me to sign another contract? Don't you trust me?'" Pat Petronelli recalled. "So we didn't. And he paid us."

Hagler moved quickly to the top of New England amateur boxing. Along the way he acquired his signature shaved head, which he explained was partly "for luck" and partly in tribute to two shaved-head legends, Jack Johnson and Rubin "Hurricane" Carter. Unspoken but understood was Hagler's appreciation of a shaved head as a blunt instrument in the ring.

He cultivated both a menacing look and personality. "He was a pain – not the most pleasant person in those days," remembered Bill Hoar, a Massachusetts amateur boxing official.

This was the Hagler who captured the 165-pound title at the AAU nationals in May 1973, while Leonard was upset in the 139-pound final by Randy Shields, son of a Hollywood stuntman.

In victory Hagler ran around the ring and waved a small American flag as the crowd applauded. He was voted the Outstanding Fighter Award and met his childhood idol, Floyd Patterson, who had worked the CBS telecast.

Leonard did not watch Hagler's bout or his celebration. His thoughts had raced ahead to Montreal and 1976. Their paths diverged, and when they next crossed, a few years later, their alchemy began to give off heat.

CHAPTER 5

· · · · · · · · · · · · · · · · · · · ·

1979: Champion and "Victim"

Two world title bouts were fought at Caesars Palace Hotel and Casino on November 30, 1979, but only one was a main event: welterweight champion Wilfredo Benitez and challenger Sugar Ray Leonard.

The other title bout at the Las Vegas boxing mecca was a preliminary: middleweight champion Vito Antuofermo and challenger Marvin Hagler.

Both Leonard and Hagler made their first bid for a world title on the same night, in the same ring. Leonard was paid a purse that finally matched his smile – $ 1 million. Hagler got $40,000. Hagler believed his value to the card was going into Leonard's pocket, and was livid.

"What about me?" he complained to his managers and attorney. "Who is he to get a million bucks?"

Hagler had seen this before. The Hartford Civic Center had featured Leonard as the main event, in his third pro bout, in June 1977. Hagler had fought the prelim, in his 36th pro bout. Leonard was paid $40,000 while Hagler got $2,000.

"I've watched Hagler – we've fought on the same card," Leonard joked years later. "He just happened to fight on the undercard."

Leonard arrived at his first title fight a little more than 2½ years and 26 bouts into his pro career. Hagler arrived after 6½ years and 49 bouts.

Hagler now saw his career as cruelly Sisyphean, an endless tease of hard work, neglect and deprivation. He saw himself as a victim of boxing politics and life's general unfairness. A sense of injustice, reinforced by purse disparities and his prolonged slog to the top, overtook his public persona. Rooted in the psychology of his childhood, it was aggravated by the cartel-like conditions of the boxing industry. The cartel consisted of two promoters, Don King and Bob Arum, and two sanctioning bodies, the World Boxing Council, based in Mexico, and the World Boxing Association, based in Panama and Venezuela.

After the 1976 Olympics American TV networks gradually rediscovered boxing. King and Arum, who had mastered the largely corrupt politics of the sanctioning bodies, controlled the world championships. Attempts by ABC and CBS to establish their own champions ended badly. As a result the networks dealt almost exclusively with King – despite his role in ABC's tainted championship tournament – and Arum.

Fighters such as Hagler, who refused, or were not offered, promotional deals with King or Arum, were ignored by the sanctioning bodies and left out of the lush stream of TV money. It wasn't until the early 1980s that other promoters, such as Dan Duva, Murad Muhammad, and Russell Peltz, started to grab some of the TV money.

After Hagler turned pro in 1973 – and earned $50 for his first pro bout – he fought primarily in New England for three years. Though he built a 25-0-1 record, he was largely unknown. By 1976, now the father of his second son, Marvin, Jr., and renting an apartment in Brockton, Hagler wanted to move beyond paydays of $1500 to $2000. Desperate to elevate his profile, Hagler went to Philadelphia in 1976 and fought two talented local middle-weights, Bobby "Boogaloo" Watts and Willie "The Worm" Monroe. Watts took a controversial decision, while Monroe won by a wide margin. The two losses were the first of six bouts known as the "Philly Wars" on Hagler's resume. He subsequently beat Monroe in two rematches, as well as two other Philadelphia middleweights, Eugene Hart and Bennie Briscoe. But the initial losses to Watts and Monroe gave the cartel an excuse to ignore him, and delayed his advance to a title bout by at least a year. When a Don King–sponsored "champion-

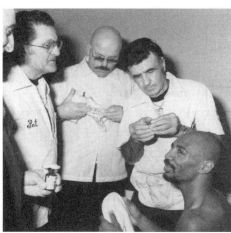

© Angie Carlino

Team Hagler: (l–r) Pat Petronelli, attorney Steve Wainwright, Goody Petronelli, Marvelous Marvin Hagler.

ship" tournament launched on ABC early in 1977, and excluded Hagler from the field of eight middleweights, his sense of victimization verged toward paranoia.

Eventually the Petronellis grasped the politics. They hired an attorney, Steven Wainwright, who enlisted the help of several Massachusetts politicians, House Speaker Thomas P. "Tip" O'Neill, Jr., Senator Edward Kennedy, and Senator Paul Tsongas, as well as Congressman Edward P. Beard of Rhode Island. The politicians, in letters to Arum, threatened federal regulation of boxing. Arum, a former assistant U.S. attorney, got the message and agreed to promote Hagler.

By February of 1979 Hagler had fought more top-10 fighters than any other middleweight. The harsh New England winter found Hagler training at the tip of Cape Cod, in Provincetown, Mass., both a gay enclave and a Portuguese-American fishing town. Each dawn he arose, pulled on Army boots, and ran among beach dunes, punching at the frigid salt air, sunlight glinting off his shaved head. Provinc-

© Angie Carlino

Marvelous Marvin Hagler training at the Provincetown Inn.

etown, austere and isolated, was a reflection of Hagler's inner Spartan. Bertha and the children were not allowed to visit, and Hagler kept to himself in a quiet wing of the semi-deserted Provincetown Inn, where his workouts were held. He was not entirely a recluse. After his morning run he strolled through town, chatted with storekeepers, and relaxed at a coffee shop amongst residents, gay and straight. Precious few were such moments, when he did not brood about his unjust fate.

"Look at all that money those Olympic kids got, look at all that money tennis players get," Hagler told Michael Katz of the *New York Times*. "Leon Spinks got a title shot after seven fights. Some guys have fought for the title four times. This is my 45th fight and I still haven't gotten one and I know all I'm going to get is one. I'm too good for my own good."

Pressured by Washington, Arum guided Hagler to his long-awaited title bout. His opponent was Vito Antuofermo, an energetic awkward fireplug with skin like tissue paper who had won the middleweight championship in June. Six and a half years after turning pro, Hagler fought for the championship in his 50th pro bout.

In a historical perspective, Hagler was approximately on schedule. It's a fact that he waited longer than his contemporaries in other weight divisions. Leonard made it as a welterweight in 26 bouts, Thomas Hearns as a welterweight in 29 bouts, and Larry Holmes as a heavyweight in 28 bouts.

But in other weight divisions there were two world titles up for grabs – from the WBC and the WBA – thus twice as many title bouts. The middleweight title had been unified for most of the 1970s; thus there were half as many title bouts available for Hagler and other middleweight contenders.

Philadelphia promoter Russell Peltz rejected the notion that Hagler was unfairly held back.

"I know there is a lot of talk that Marvin didn't get breaks early, but that's not really true," said Peltz. "I had four black middleweights in Philly and they were all tough guys...but only one of them, Bennie Briscoe, fought for the title. It was harder to get a title fight in those days...and Marvin didn't really hit his peak until the late 70s. The only place where Marvin had a tough time is when he got excluded from the Don King tournament. That was outrageous. But if that tournament had never come along, Marvin was still right on schedule. You couldn't get a title fight in those days with 15 fights. You had to have 35 or 40."

Antuofermo was an opponent of limited talent whom Hagler should easily have defeated. Early in the fight that appeared to be the case, as his switch-hitting attack confused Antuofermo and opened cuts under both eyes.

Yet, inexplicably, in the middle rounds Hagler let down. Antuofermo overcame a 5½-inch reach disadvantage by leaping at Hagler and landing with both hands. Hagler backed up and found himself in uncharted territory against the ropes. From the 11th round on it was a slugging match, and though Hagler rocked Antuofermo in the 15th the round went to Antuofermo.

Most ringside media thought Hagler won by a comfortable margin, and the referee, Mills Lane, told Hagler to face the photographers for the moment when he would raise his hand. But that moment never came. The judges called it a draw, and allowed Antuofermo to retain the title. The judge who voted for Hagler, Duane Ford, was so upset at the outcome that he later vomited outside the Caesars sports pavilion.

"The challenger must win decisively to become champion," a Nevada official told Hagler.

"In my heart I still believe I'm the middleweight champion," Hagler said. "If the judges knew anything about boxing they'd have felt the same way."

Broken-hearted and embittered, Hagler returned to Brockton and despaired of a second chance. The world was not fair to black shaved-head southpaw fighters – he was sure of it. He told a friend, "From now on I'm taking no prisoners."

1979: World Champion

Compared to Hagler, Leonard's ascent to the championship level was pre-ordained. His path was smoother because he had what Hagler lacked – an Olympic gold medal.

He converted his "million dollar smile" into hard cash, but not without collateral damage to people and principles.

Foremost was Ray, Jr., born on November 22, 1973. Juanita was two months shy of 16; Leonard was 17, and both were in high school. They agreed that Juanita would raise the baby under her father's roof while he continued to live with his family, an arrangement Leonard had encouraged to abet his Olympic quest. The decision was practical, since neither had an income and neither family could afford to set them up on their own. But the practical effect was that Leonard's routine of school and boxing did not change, while Juanita had to drop out of school and go to work.

She worked at fast food restaurants, and in the summer at the service station managed by her father. Juanita cleaned windshields, changed oil and tires, and pumped gas, and when she went home she took care of Ray, Jr. Part of her paycheck supplemented her father's household budget, and part of it went to Leonard.

"Ray, with his responsibilities, was not able to work a lot of the time," Juanita recalled. "I had to help him out, as well as his family, you know, when they got into some bad situations."

Leonard did not contribute financially, nor was he much of a presence as a father, from Juanita's perspective.

"He was so dedicated that I think fatherhood never really became a big thing to him at that time," Juanita said.

Even Leonard eventually would admit he had "neglected" Ray, Jr. Boxing came between him and his son, but boxing was not solely responsible. Dick Wilkinson, whose own marriage had failed, detected something familiar and unsettling in Leonard. "Dick saw things – himself maybe," said Ollie Dunlap. "He knew that when Ray left the house he was on the prowl."

Leonard won both the national Golden Gloves and AAU titles in 1974. His star ascended in 1975 as he won another national AAU title and a gold medal in the Pan American Games. He got airtime on ABC's popular Saturday afternoon show, "Wide World of Sports," and caught the attention of Cosell, the bombastic and influential broadcaster. Cosell had ridden to fame in the 1960s on the coattails of Muhammad Ali, with whom he shared a crackling and comedic rapport. Now, with Ali's career in its twilight, Cosell saw Ali's image in Leonard. He also saw an Ali-like charisma to drive TV ratings.

But a funny thing happened on Leonard's way to Montreal – he almost did not get there, nearly victimized by his own artful dodging. After fibbing to Olympic officials in his failed attempt to qualify in 1972, he manipulated the process in 1976.

One of the qualifying routes was the national Golden Gloves, a tournament Leonard had won for three straight years. But in March 1976 he withdrew before the quarterfinal round, ostensibly because of a cut lip. His quarterfinal opponent was to be Ronnie Shields, a tough 139-pounder from Fort Worth.

"Shields was really sharp and Ray didn't look too good," recalled Emanuel Steward, then coach and mastermind of the fast-rising Kronk Gym team from Detroit. "That's why Dave pulled Ray out."

Another qualifying route was the AAU national, which Leonard had won the previous two years. But Leonard did not compete, oddly enough. No explanations surfaced in the print media. What happened, at least according to Steward, is that Leonard was suspended, or was threatened with suspension, by the AAU for signing up to compete in a region outside his home region, Potomac.

"There was another boy in Potomac who was a problem," Steward said. "So Ray registered in another region and got caught."

Details clouded over time. Steward thought the violation occurred in the Tennessee region, where another 139-pounder, Milton "Pete" Seward, was considered an Olympic prospect. The record is clear, however, that Leonard did not compete in the AAU nationals, at a time when he needed to.

Now just one option remained – maybe. Leonard could advance through an Eastern Regional qualifying tournament. Only there wasn't one – nobody had stepped forth to host it. Scant motivation had existed, since it was assumed the best fighters would advance in the Golden Gloves and AAU.

Jacobs, anxious and worried, called Steward.

"There's one chance for Ray to make the Olympic team," Jacobs pleaded. "If you can get the Eastern Regional trials."

Steward had been an admirer of Leonard's for years, so much so that the walls of the Kronk Gym were plastered with his photos. Thrown together on the amateur circuit, they had struck up a friendship, though Steward was 12 years Leonard's senior.

Steward agreed to organize the event and quickly raised money. Jacobs agreed that Leonard would train at the Kronk, an overheated basement gym in a Depression-era municipal building.

Steward's team welcomed Leonard in May 1976 as though he were a reigning world champion. Among the Kronk fighters dazzled by Leonard's panache was 17-year-old Thomas Hearns, a beanpole 132-pounder whose own Olympic bid had been cut short by a nose injury.

Hearns was not among the Kronk fighters who sparred with Leonard – his turn would come later.

Leonard seized this final opportunity. He won the Eastern Regional tournament, and then beat Shields in the Olympic trials to win his berth on the U.S. team.

Thus, when Cosell opened ABC's telecast of the Summer Games on July 17, 1976, he chose one athlete, Leonard, to stand by his side at the center of Olympic Village.

Leonard's performance justified ABC's spotlight. He beat a Swede, Russian, East German, and a Pole, and he won convincingly despite throbbing pain in his chronically sore hands. In reaching the gold medal round Leonard displayed a range of styles and tactics, and wisely tempered his flourishes – smiling, shuffling and bolo punching – to appease international judges. His success was magnified by the success of his teammates. Leon Spinks (175 pounds), his brother Michael Spinks (160 pounds), Howard Davis (132 pounds) and Leo Randolph (118 pounds) all advanced to the finals, and won gold.

Ultimately it wasn't Leonard's ring performance that elevated his celebrity above the others – it was his personality. In his interviews with Cosell and print media he came across as an All-American boy, fresh, earnest, articulate, respectful, and slightly impish. He was the Chamber of Commerce booster who unfurled the red-and-white flag of Prince George's County. Animated in the ring, Leonard pretended to pat his hair back into place when an opponent narrowly missed with a haymaker. The arrival from Maryland of a rented camper with his parents, Juanita, brother Roger, sisters Sharon and Sandy, Jacobs, and a couple of friends added texture to his personal story. More depth was added by Leonard's decision to tape a photo of Juanita to the socks he wore into the ring.

In the Olympic final he defeated a rugged Cuban southpaw, Andres Aldama, who took three standing eight counts. Leonard's gold gave American boxers five for the first time since 1952.

In a jubilant aftermath, as Cosell held a microphone to his face, Leonard made a surprise announcement.

"I've fought my last fight," Leonard said. "My journey has ended. My dream is fulfilled."

It was the first of many retirements for Leonard. He was exhausted, his knuckles were bruised and swollen, and he wanted a break from boxing. He rode back to Maryland in the rented camper and was greeted by a police escort, fawning public officials and a neighborhood celebration.

Media engulfed the Leonard home on Barlowe Road. Leonard told reporters he had enjoyed his moment of glory and was proud to be in the record books, but that pro boxing was not in his future.

"I'll never be a professional fighter – I promise you that," he said. "It's time I started a new life."

He recalled Ali's advice to put education ahead of boxing and said he planned to get a degree at nearby University of Maryland–College Park. He thought he might follow Dunlap into youth work.

His gold medal, he said, belonged to the Palmer Park community.

"With my girl friend and family in Montreal to cheer

me on, I couldn't let them down," he said. "But now I want to set an example for all the kids in the streets."

But Leonard's career as an example-setter was short-lived. Two days after his return from Montreal, on August 5, 1976, the *Washington Star* bannered a front-page headline: "Sugar Ray's Paternity Suit."

The story detailed a paternity suit filed against Leonard by the county. The suit was triggered by a food stamp application submitted by Juanita, who had been receiving county child support payments for a year. Mandating the suit was a new law intended to determine if unwed fathers could support their children.

Juanita had not known her food stamp application automatically triggered a paternity suit, and Leonard had not even known she had submitted it. Both were caught off guard by the article, which seemed to mock the notion of the loving couple projected by Leonard at Montreal, not to mention the relationship of Leonard with his county, whose flag he had waved before a worldwide audience.

The irony was more than cruel, and when media descended once again on Palmer Park, Leonard reacted with indignation.

"Here I bring the county flag to the Olympics and give them their share of glory and what do I get – a paternity suit," Leonard sniffed.

He explained that he had not "denied" Ray, Jr., was proud of him, and fully intended to contribute to his support.

"I wasn't working because I was training hard and in school," Leonard said. "I was always occupied with something else. I didn't have time to help them the way I wanted to. But you know, this was a dream I had to fulfill even though I neglected Ray somewhat.

"The worst thing is that all the kids here look up to me, and then this thing blows up in my face. It will destroy me. I wouldn't want the kids to see me in a different light...all I can say is I'm sorry. I wish it hadn't happened at this particular time."

An ugly uproar ensued. Leonard and his supporters questioned the public airing of his private life and inferred that the story had racist overtones. County executives, who had supplied Leonard with the flag, pointed fingers at the county attorney for bringing the suit. Plenty of everyday fans turned against Leonard, perhaps feeling suckered and betrayed by his display of Juanita's photo at Montreal. He received hate mail.

Product endorsement offers dried up. Even as another Olympic hero, decathlon gold medalist Bruce Jenner, reaped lucrative national endorsements, Leonard's were local and modest. Some Leonard confidantes believed Jenner's face was on a Wheaties cereal box, and not Leonard's, because of racism, pure and simple.

Soon Leonard's problems compounded. His mother, who had been ill before the Olympics, suffered a minor heart attack. His father, who had been docked pay when he traveled to Montreal, fell ill with spinal meningitis. With both unable to work, their financial situation became perilous.

Leonard was affected by his parents' plight. Though aloof as a father and boyfriend, he was a devoted son.

© Ollie Dunlap

Sugar Ray Leonard, left, and attorney Michael G. Trainer, early 1980s.

He needed money to help them, as well as to support Little Ray. The obvious solution was to turn pro.

It was then Leonard met Michael G. Trainer, a puckish, combative 35-year-old attorney who knew virtually nothing about boxing and a lot about fighting. Trainer came into Leonard's life to give advice on a paternity suit, and stayed to construct and pilot the financial juggernaut known as Sugar Ray Leonard, Inc.

Adopted at birth, Trainer grew up in Bethesda, put himself through University of Maryland Law School, clerked for a Circuit Court judge, and built a practice in real estate, drunk driving, personal injury, and divorce. He took pride in being self-made, and was skeptical of others who started, as he put it, "with a leg up." Married and father to two daughters, Trainer enjoyed beer, cigarettes, golf, and soft-leather loafers worn without socks.

Trainer's philosophy was reflected in the changing economics of sports. Free agency had come to Major League Baseball in 1976. Andy Messersmith had landed a three-year $1 million deal – a staggering amount – with Ted Turner's Atlanta Braves. Reggie Jackson, Bobby

Grich, Joe Rudi, Don Baylor, and Rollie Fingers played without contracts in order to become free agents after the season. The notion of free agency resonated with Trainer, who had opened his own practice two years after passing the bar.

Soon after he met Leonard, Trainer imparted his philosophy of self-ownership.

"He had an offer on the table from Abe Pollin, who ran the Capital Centre, for $250,000, and a 50 percent cut," Trainer recalled. "I asked Ray, 'will it bother you if after you make $500,000 and he gets his money back he will take half of what you earn?' And he said, 'yes.'

"I said, 'you can do that, or go into business yourself and fight and keep all of it.' He came back in about a week and said, 'I want to go into business for myself.'"

It was revolutionary for boxing, a big new idea that undercut decades of custom and practice. Boxers always had worked for managers, trainers, and promoters. Managers and trainers usually took a combined 33 percent of the boxer's earnings, if not more, while promoters claimed all or most of the profit above the boxer's fixed fee.

Trainer's idea was that Leonard would hire a manager and trainer at fixed salaries far less than the customary rate. He would act as his own promoter and contract out the operational and marketing functions at a fixed fee. Under this system, profit belonged to Leonard.

Free agency resonated with Leonard, too. Shortly after the Olympics he had visited Yankee Stadium and had been cornered by promoter Don King in a restroom. King, a former numbers racketeer who had stomped a man to death on a Cleveland sidewalk, and served four years in an Ohio prison before becoming a promoter, tried to recruit Leonard. But Leonard scurried away feeling as though he needed to shower. The other major promoter, Bob Arum, held no more appeal, nor did any of the second-tier promoters, but it was more than that. Leonard's alter ego, Sugar Ray, was a free lancer by inclination. Sugar Ray needed room to maneuver, and he needed to be his own boss.

Leonard announced his decision publicly on October 12, 1976. Twenty-four local investors created a pool of $21,000 to finance his start-up. Trainer called the group "a community-oriented investment organization" that would take only a small percentage of Leonard's earnings and eventually enable him to stand on his own feet.

"I'm doing it for my parents," Leonard said. "They're kind of down now and I'm capable of lifting them back up. I want to put them in a good financial position.

"It won't be like I'm a piece of property with someone saying, 'OK, you fight there, there and there.'"

The rest of the team fell quickly into place. Charlie Brotman, a cheerful public relations veteran, was brought in to organize Leonard's appearances and media requests. Brotman had worked for the old Washington Senators before they departed the capital in 1961, and subsequently for failed pro basketball and soccer franchises.

Brotman was asked to recruit a manager who could navigate Leonard to a championship – someone to select opponents and parse the arcane politics of the sanctioning bodies. He zeroed in on three veterans – Eddie

Futch, Gil Clancy, and
Angelo Dundee – with
sterling credentials.
Dundee, 55, ultimately
was chosen because he
was willing to let Leon-
ard train with Jacobs in
Palmer Park. Dundee,
of course, was Ali's
corner man, and had
worked with eight other
champions. His hir-
ing gave Leonard even
more credibility.

© Ollie Dunlap
Trainer Angelo Dundee (left),
Leonard, trainer Janks Morton
(right), and publicist Charlie
Brotman (kneeling).

Trainer's strategy was to maximize rewards and minimize risk. Dundee was under strict orders not to over-
match Leonard. Meanwhile, Trainer prospected for the
best offers from TV networks and grassroots promoters.

Leonard's first pro bout, on Feb. 5, 1977, televised by
CBS, was held at the Baltimore Civic Center. Though pro
boxing had been dormant in Baltimore for 20 years, city
officials recruited the bout and pledged money, so certain
were they of Leonard's appeal. The fight was advertised
on billboards, posters, and the backs of buses. Leonard
even sent a telegram to President Jimmy Carter, in office
for less than a month, and asked him to attend. "If you
are unable to attend please tune in CBS television," the
telegram read.

The night before the fight Leonard took Juanita and

Ray, Jr., to the film *Rocky*, which would soon win the Oscar for Best Picture of 1976.

Dundee found an opponent who evoked the fictional "Rocky" – Luis "The Bull" Vega, a squarely built Puerto Rican expatriate. Leonard, at 140 pounds, drubbed the hapless Vega but could not drop him en route to a six-round decision. The event drew 10,270, and the live gate, along with $10,000 in TV fees, pushed Leonard's take to $40,000. Vega was paid $650.

Leonard paid off his original investors each with $40 interest, and became the sole owner of Sugar Ray Leonard, Inc. He was able to rent an apartment for himself, Ray, Jr., and Juanita, who was enrolled at a local community college. Leonard turned 21. He had been a man for several years, and now he could pay his bills like one.

In his rise to the top, Leonard chose marketability over credibility. In 1978 he notched six knockouts in 11 bouts, and fought in outposts such as Dayton, New Haven, Utica, Providence, Portland, Me., and Springfield, Mass., usually before crowds of 5,000 or more. In April 1978 he fought at the Capital Centre in Landover, Md., and drew 15,272, the largest indoor boxing crowd ever in Maryland.

Meanwhile, Trainer played the networks against one another and cut lucrative new deals with ABC and HBO. In January 1979 Leonard broke his own attendance record, drawing 19,743 to the Capital Centre for his bout with Johnny Gant of Washington. The bout was billed as a local turf war, though Leonard had little trouble en route to an 8th-round TKO. Indeed, Gant, a respectable journeyman and a ranked welterweight, was only a tad better than most of Leonard's opponents during his build-up period.

In guiding Leonard to the top, Dundee had rather easily fulfilled his mission to find pliable opponents. Only once did Dundee stumble. Marcos Geraldo, a Mexican middleweight (160 pounds), hurt Leonard in the early going and extended him the 10-round distance. Trainer was furious at Dundee after Geraldo nearly derailed Sugar Ray Leonard, Inc.

But Leonard had yet to be tested by a championship-quality opponent. Some perceived him as a TV creation. He had fought 12 times on ABC, three times on HBO, twice on CBS, and once on NBC, and had appeared as an analyst on CBS and ABC boxing shows. Cameras loved him, but he needed a world title for validation, not to mention leverage for future bonanzas.

On his way up Leonard neatly sidestepped the two best fighters in his division – Roberto Duran and Thomas Hearns. He also avoided a skillful veteran, Carlos Palomino, who had lost the WBC title to Benitez in January 1979.

Pipino Cuevas, a hard-hitting Mexican knockout artist, held the WBA title. Either title would do, but Leonard chose the safer opponent, Benitez, a deft boxer who possessed little of Cuevas' punching power, or for that matter, Leonard's.

Benitez had won a 140-pound title at age 17 before he won his welterweight title. The 21-year-old Puerto Rican had a 37-0-1 record when he signed to fight Leonard.

On the eve of the fight Leonard received a call from Ali.

"None of our stuff," Ali said.

No hot-dogging, he meant. Scoring judges would take a dim view of such antics against a world champion.

Forewarned, Leonard was all business in a tense tactical match between mirror-image boxers who, oddly enough, fought flat-footed. Leonard floored Benitez in the 3rd, amassed a lead in the middle rounds, and staggered Benitez in the 11th. Benitez mounted a comeback in the 12th, 13th and 14th rounds, but made the mistake of taunting Leonard with a grin at the onset of the 15th. The final round was a slugfest, until Leonard gained the upper hand in the final 30 seconds, dropped Benitez, and forced a stoppage with six seconds remaining.

Afterward, Leonard reminded the press, "People said I was just a Hollywood actor."

He returned to Maryland and, tit-for-tat, declined a White House invitation from Jimmy Carter, who had declined an invitation to his first pro bout.

No longer a "Hollywood actor," but a world champion, with earnings of $4 million, Leonard decided to marry Juanita. Theirs would not be a Hollywood wedding, although it was preceded by a tinseltown trope: a prenuptial agreement.

The wedding, on January 19, 1980, took place at the First Baptist Church of Highland Park in Landover, Md., with six-year-old Ray Jr., as ring-bearer. The standing-room-only crowd included a *Washington Post* society reporter, who wrote that Leonard "looked dazed but remained on his feet" as he left the altar.

They honeymooned in Los Angeles and Las Vegas.

Then they returned to oversee construction of a new home on eight acres in suburban Potomac, Md. It included a sauna, basketball and tennis courts, basement gym, swimming pool, and five bedrooms. Juanita drove a new Fiat convertible while Leonard tooled around in a new black Mercedes sedan.

Life was good. Leonard was at the top of the Fight Game, confident, secure, infinitely clever, and yet, unbeknownst to him, vulnerable. He was about to enter a subtler realm of boxing.

CHAPTER 6

·····················

1980: Duran

A CROWDED MONTREAL SIDEWALK was the stage for a remarkable pas de deux on an afternoon in June 1980. Two groups of pedestrians converged. One was Ray Leonard, his wife, and entourage. The other included a man whose fierce visage, it would be written, "reminded some of Che Guevara, others of Charles Manson."

Juanita Leonard was startled to find Roberto Duran's flat impenetrable black eyes locked on hers. Was he looking at her? He was.

"I keel your husband," Duran snarled.

To make sure she heard he repeated himself.

"I keel your husband."

In the next instant Duran and his group moved on. Juanita was stricken. Leonard's jaw was on his chest. Then his blood began to rise. Duran had besmirched his honor.

"This went on for four or five days – you could see

Ray losing his composure," recalled Ollie Dunlap. "This was the first time Ray had the Fight Game put on him. Duran worked him."

Leonard fought Duran on June 20, 1980, lost a close but unanimous decision, and earned his graduate degree in pugilism.

Duran was a picaresque character, one that a novelist or screenwriter might have invented. By 1980 his career was in its second act, in his late prime, at the age of 29.

Raised by a single mother in Panama City's poorest slum, Duran had known a depth of poverty beyond Hagler or Leonard's imagination. His was banana republic poverty, with tropical heat and mosquitoes and the persistent ache of an empty stomach.

The facts of Duran's early years, blurred by his own embellishment, survive as semi-myth. At 12 Duran shined shoes, varnished furniture, hawked the daily newspaper, sang and danced in saloons for loose change, and foraged for food. One day he followed his older brother to a local gym and took up boxing.

Soon he became a street brawler, and was expelled from third grade, at 13, for pushing another student down a stairwell. He knocked out five men in their 20s who eyed his girl at a dance, and was jailed overnight with his victims – one of whom was out cold until the morning.

Yet another story – Duran's favorite – placed him at a country fair. He tried to impress a girl but had no money to buy whiskey. A fellow challenged Duran to a wager – $2 and two bottles of whiskey – if he could knock out a nearby horse. Duran planted a hard one behind the horse's ear, it toppled, and he won the bet. But the punch ripped his hand open to the bone. He deferred medical attention to stay with the girl, but alas, he did not get a single kiss.

All of these incidents made Duran a local character, but they did not put food in his belly. By now he was one of Panama's best amateur boxers, and one of its dirtiest. He liked to hit low, butt, thumb, and knee. When amateur officials left him off an international team, for fear of an incident, he turned pro. At 16, in the rat-infested port of Colon, he won a four-round decision over Carlos Mendoza, and was paid $25.

Duran debuted in New York on Sept. 13, 1971, on the undercard of a lightweight title bout, and knocked out Benny Huertas in the 1st round. "Duran hardly worked up a sweat," wrote Vic Ziegel of the *New York Post*. "A good thing, too, because he didn't bother to shower." Duran hated the line, and remembered it when Ziegel came to interview him in 1980.

By June 1972 he was ready for lightweight champion Ken Buchanan. In promoting the bout, Madison Square Garden played up Duran's background as a Panama City street fighter. Duran embellished the role, spewed Spanish invective at Buchanan at the weigh-in, and predicted a 9th-round knockout.

Duran dominated Buchanan and stopped him in the 13th round. The bout ended in controversy as a downed Buchanan writhed and twitched involuntarily, after a low blow and a knee to the groin.

Over the next six years Duran defended his title 12

times and became a virtual folk hero in Panama, known as "Manos de Piedra" (Hands of Stone), celebrated as the best "pound-for-pound" fighter in the world. He paid no taxes, had a military jeep at his disposal, and was a friend of Panamanian strong man Gen. Omar Torrijos. He kept six cars in his driveway and a 680-pound pet lion in his backyard. He was married, and a father, and supported his mother and untold family members. When he was not home, frequently, his diversions were women, food and drink.

"Women and the glass – those are my only two drugs," Duran told reporters, though he might have included, "fork and knife."

By 1978 Duran had eaten himself out of the 135-pound division and could see a virtual feast, Leonard, rising at 147 pounds. It made perfect sense to become a 147-pounder – he could eat more and earn more. In June 1979 Duran manhandled former welterweight champion, Carlos Palomino, and waited for Leonard's dethroning of Benitez.

The Leonard-Duran bout was arranged early in 1980 after a tense negotiation that included the commander of the Panamanian National Guard interceding on Duran's behalf. Trainer controlled the process, chose Montreal's Olympic Stadium as the site, and installed both Arum and King as co-promoters. Leonard's purse was approximately $10 million, largely due to closed-circuit TV revenue, much of it from Duran's Latino fans. Duran's purse was $1.5 million, ten times more than he ever had made, but puny in comparison.

Once the fighters arrived in Montreal, the tables turned. Duran controlled the process, in a way Leonard had not experienced or imagined. In every sense of the Fight Game, Leonard had met his match.

First, Duran captured the locals. Les Quebecois were drawn to his warmth, flamboyance, and Spanish language. Any language was preferable to English after a Quebec-wide vote to secede from the Canadian federation had lost decisively less than a month before.

Large midday crowds attended Duran's workouts at a downtown shopping mall. Duran blew kisses and pressed flesh, and picked up shreds of French and tossed them at fans in a comical helium-injected voice: "Oui Oui monsieur" and "Parlez-vous Francais?" When a fan shouted "Leonardo Leonardo!" he broke into an impromptu pantomime and flew around the ring like a chicken.

Les Quebecois were cool to Leonard, the incorporated fighter who drove prices for mid-range seats – from $75 to $300 – nearly out of reach. He was surprised because he had won his gold medal in Montreal in 1976. The city had embraced Leonard and his family as one of the Game's feel-good stories. But now Duran's workouts drew larger crowds and local media doted on him. Leonard was unsettled. Public rejection and indifference were new to his psyche.

Leonard speculated that he had become an object of envy.

"These people don't really hate me," he said. "They just don't want to see me succeed. I guess for some there has to be a flaw, something wrong, something negative."

Meanwhile, Duran's weight was under control, not always a given. He walked the Montreal streets with bodyguards whose job was to keep him out of the pastry shops and bistros – and in the path of Leonard and Juanita.

Three days before the bout Duran was summoned to a hospital due to an irregular EKG reading on a heart test. For half a day, until a new test came back negative, Leonard worried about a cancellation and the loss of $10 million. He wondered if Duran had manipulated the scare.

Later that same day Leonard met with Charlie Brotman, his publicity director. Brotman had a list of canned questions for the media horde and wanted Leonard's answers. Brotman's first question was, "How are you going to fight Duran?"

"Flat-footed," Leonard replied.

Brotman blanched. "What?"

"I'm going to beat Duran at his own game," Leonard said. "I'm faster than he is, I can hit as hard as he does, I can take a punch as well as he can. That's the way I'm going to fight."

The notion had taken hold, against conventional wisdom, common sense, and Sweet Science. The bout was predicated on contrasting styles: Duran was supposed to brawl, Leonard was supposed to box. By "sticking and moving," Leonard could exploit his speed and reach advantage. Except that now he wanted to brawl.

A ceremonial weigh-in was held at the shopping mall a day before the bout. Juanita saw a woman gesture at her.

"Who's giving me the finger?" Juanita asked

Duran's wife, Felicidad, she was told.

"Real nice," said Juanita. "I'll just smile back."

Now Leonard was to fight a guy with a bad heart whose wife gave his wife the finger.

In boxing usually the legs go first, then the body and head. But in Leonard's case it was his judgment.

The first meaningful punch, thrown by Duran 30 seconds into the bout, caught Leonard on his protective cup. Welcome to my world, Duran seemed to say. Welcome to the fetid, putrid, remorseless Panamanian slum I come from, pretty boy.

Fifteen rounds later, at the final bell, Leonard extended his glove toward his tormentor. Tap it, you little devil, Leonard seemed to say. You mangled my face and mauled my ribs but you didn't break me. Tap my glove – this is what civilized people do.

Their bout virtually started with a low blow and ended with Duran slapping away Leonard's glove outstretched in sportsmanship. In between were 15 rounds of boxing and brawling at a pace rarely seen in the ring. So intense was the action, and so subtle the skills of Duran and Leonard that scoring was difficult for the three European judges, and description elusive for media.

It was not a bout of specific blows. Rather, it was a cartoon blur of fists, feet, elbows and knees, pell-mell, back and forth, purposeful, iron-willed, relentless and clever. Ultimately, Leonard's tactics played into Duran's strengths, and Duran won a close but unanimous 15-round decision.

Afterward, HBO commentator Ferdie Pacheco, who

spoke Spanish, stuck a microphone in Duran's face and asked him how he had won. Duran fairly screamed his answer.

"He says he knew he would win," Pacheco translated. "He is more of a man. He is more strong."

1980: Hagler in London

Marvin Hagler dropped to his knees in exultation and gratitude. The next instant projectiles of plastic bottles and beer cans sizzled past his shaved head. Before Hagler could react, a human shield – Goody and Pat Petronelli, attorney Steven Wainwright, and brother Robbie Sims – formed above him. Soon London police escorted the new middleweight champion from the ring to a secured room.

Hooligan fans rioted on September 27, 1980, at London's indoor Wembley Stadium, after Hagler stopped England's Alan Minter in a 3rd-round TKO. They responded to Hagler's victory with a barrage of projectiles and jeers. Nobody was hurt, including Leonard, at ringside for HBO.

Minter had lifted the title from Antuofermo in June. Hagler had arrived in London still angry over the draw in Las Vegas, and determined to circumvent the scoring judges. He had held up his two fists, and said, "This is "K" and this is "O". To a friend, Tony Petronelli, Hagler confided, "He's going to have to kill me to beat me."

Neo-racist coverage by the British press had depicted Hagler as a dark ghetto apparition intent on mugging

Minter. Hagler was "a fighting desperado from the wrong side of the tracks who fights dirty – with his fists or his tongue," according to the *Sunday People*. He was "panther-like…the kind of face that would convert most people into instant pacifists," wrote the London Express.

Minter, from the London suburb of Crawley, looked more like an English butler or thespian than a boxer. Formerly a brawler, Minter's style had changed after an opponent, Angelo Jacopucci, died as a result of their 1978 bout. He had used a tactical approach to twice defeat Antuofermo – the second time in an 8th-round TKO.

Twelve thousand fans crowded the arena to see Minter bring honor to the Union Jack. Instead, they saw a vintage Hagler, precise and remorseless. He forced Minter to engage, and in the 1st round he split open Minter's wax-paper skin in two places. Another cut opened in the second. Six cuts were open, and Minter's face a mask of blood, when the fight was stopped at 1:45 in the 3rd round.

In the fan riot that followed, Minter's two championship belts were forgotten. Routinely, the belts would be strapped around the waist of the new champion, but a ceremony was impossible under the circumstances. Hagler could not win for winning. Even when he finally won the long-awaited title his moment of triumph was co-opted.

Hagler left the arena under police escort, returned to his hotel, and partied into the next morning, and the next day, and the next. Hagler savored a drink when he wasn't in training, and now that he was middleweight champion, he indulged. He and photographer Angie Carlino shared a bottle of Jim Beam before "cleaning out everything in his room," Carlino recalled. When Hagler flew home a police motorcade whisked him from Logan Airport in Boston to a rally of 3500 fans at Brockton City Hall.

He hit all the right notes. Marciano had put Brockton on the map, he said, and he intended to keep it there. He kissed Rocky's mother and thanked her family for supporting him. He thanked Bertha, Mae, the Petronellis, and God. To the young people, Hagler said, "Go after your dream – it will come true if you want it bad enough."

Two weeks later the two championship belts arrived. In a special ceremony, Jersey Joe Walcott, the old warhorse dethroned as heavyweight champion by Marciano in 1952, placed the belts around his waist. That Hagler had to wait to obtain his prized belts – after fleeing an ugly mob – fit conveniently into the aggrieved narrative of his career. In time, the London bout

© Angie Carlino

Hagler's most prized possessions were his two championship belts. He saw them as validation of his long slog to the top.

would be remembered more for the hooligan fans than the savage demolition of Minter.

1980: No Mas

At center ring Ray Charles sang "America the Beautiful" while lit by the 100-watt smile of his namesake, Ray Charles Leonard. The blind vocalist made his way to Leonard and hugged him.

As the two Rays embraced at the Louisiana Superdome on November 25, 1980, the champion, Duran, watched from the opposite corner. There would be no love for Duran on this fateful night.

The rematch showcased Leonard's resolve and cleverness. But his journey from Montreal to New Orleans had not been easy.

Immediately after his loss in Montreal, Leonard's face was somebody else's – a funhouse mirror face. He was a mass of sores and swollen appendages. His head was lumpy and knotted and his back was raw with rope burns. Duran's right hands and the rubbing of Duran's head during clinches made his left ear hideously swollen and gnarled. Though a doctor drained it, it was tender and raw, and Leonard envisioned himself an old palooka with cauliflower ears.

Leonard's first inclination was to call it a career. Indeed, he told the media, "This is it – I can't go on," a statement generally interpreted to be his second retirement.

Juanita's position was clear – she hated boxing and Montreal had been an ordeal for her. Juanita asked him why he had fought as he did, and his answer – "I had something to prove – they were saying I couldn't take a punch" – did not comfort her.

Common sense told him to quit and preserve his health. Cleveland Denny, who fought on the undercard in Montreal, was on life-support and soon would die from the punches of Canadian Gaetan Hart. Ali himself was brain damaged, though it was not yet acknowledged. Another beating could send Leonard in the same direction. His financial future was secure after his record $10 million payday. Common sense told Leonard to cash out.

But a restorative vacation in Hawaii healed his body and spirit and made him resolve to continue. He wasn't convinced Duran was the better fighter, and he didn't want to be pitied as the guy driven into retirement by Duran.

Leonard knew from reliable sources that Duran had celebrated throughout the summer and was bloated and sodden. On the assumption that Duran needed extended conditioning, Leonard and Trainer pushed for a rematch that was sooner rather than later. Duran preferred to wait until the spring, but could not risk losing a $9 million payday if Leonard changed his mind. Early in October the two sides announced the November 25 date. Duran had seven weeks to reverse the damage of his three-month party.

Conditioning was not a problem for Leonard – he had been in the gym most of the summer. His biggest distraction was longtime trainer, Dave Jacobs, who was unhappy about his compensation and his secondary role, to Dundee, in the corner. Jacobs lobbied for a tune-up bout before a rematch with Duran. Leonard was torn between his history with Jacobs and his bottom-line philosophy. When Jacobs would not relent, he fired him.

The firing was chilling proof of Leonard's business resolve. At a press conference Leonard was asked what Jacobs' absence meant to him. "One less check to write," Leonard said, without a flicker of emotion. Veteran reporters were taken aback. "That was about as cold and callous as a person could be," recalled Thom Greer, who wrote for the *Philadelphia Daily News*. Dave Kindred, who wrote for the *Washington Post*, said, "That's the working image of Leonard in my mind."

"People look at Ray sometime and say, 'oh, he's a nice kid,' little smile and everything," recalled older brother Kenny Leonard. "But Ray got something inside of him, you know, is terrible. It's a complete dark side."

Duran struggled to drop from 180 pounds to 147, and virtually starved for three days prior to the weigh-in. On the morning of the fight, after he made weight, the famished champion tore into several steaks and various fruits, vegetables, and liquids. When he climbed into the ring, he looked thick, and his stomach lacked the tone it had in Montreal.

From the opening bell it was clear Montreal would not be duplicated. Leonard was light on his feet as he circled and darted. When Duran lunged, Leonard was gone. When Duran bulled Leonard to the ropes, he spun away. By the 3rd round a pattern emerged. As Duran chased, he repeatedly walked into stiff left jabs. When he occasionally caught up, Leonard was faster in the flurries. Duran managed a couple of flashes of energy, and eked out two close rounds on the scorecards, but he was not competitive.

The 7th round produced a remarkable spectacle. So

comfortable was Leonard that he began to mug and clown. As Duran plodded in pursuit, Leonard craned forward his face as if to say "hit me if you can." Leonard wiggled his shoulders, and spun his feet in a shuffle. When Duran managed to close the distance Leonard sharply out-punched him. Finally, Leonard wound up his right hand for a bolo punch, and as Duran lunged forward, snapped his left into Duran's face.

In the eighth Leonard stopped clowning and resumed circular movement. He darted, jabbed, and retreated. Duran's pace was slower yet. He managed one lunging attack, and his hair flew up as Leonard caught him on the way in. Leonard landed four or five solid blows in the third minute, and Duran's confusion increased.

A half-minute remained when they exchanged, near Duran's corner, and Duran got the worst of it. As referee Octavio Meyran separated a clinch, Duran turned, walked toward his corner, and waved off Leonard.

The bell had rung, spectators assumed.

Leonard came up from behind and whipped a right into his unguarded stomach and a left into his left side.

Meyran jumped in and instructed Duran to box. Leonard walked toward his own corner, arms upraised. Duran moved away from Meyran, turned a circle, and waved a glove at Leonard. It appeared he realized there had not been a bell.

Now Meyran motioned for Duran and Leonard to resume fighting. Leonard came toward Duran with gloves cocked, but once again Duran waved him off. He spoke. Meyran leaned in to hear Duran's words.

"No quiero pelear con el payaso."

I do not want to fight with this clown.

In broken English, Duran added, "I don't box anymore."

Meyran asked him why.

"No mas," Duran said. "No mas."

No more.

Meyran's right hand shot upward in a waving motion. Bout over! Leonard sprinted toward a neutral corner, leaped upon the bottom rope, and raised his arms toward the far reaches of the Superdome.

Within seconds Duran's interpreter informed media that Duran had quit because of stomach cramps.

Leonard pushed his way toward Duran, whose face already was shadowed with humiliation and regret. The two embraced, and Leonard slung an arm over Duran's shoulder, almost protectively. In the blink of an eye and the utterance of a phrase Duran had gone from champion to pariah, and Leonard from apprentice to master. Leonard had gamed Duran.

CHAPTER 7

....

1981: Hit Man

DETROIT MAYOR COLEMAN YOUNG took one look at *Ring* magazine's December 1980 cover and exploded. His profanity-laced tirade echoed throughout City Hall. "Get me Emanuel Steward," Young bellowed.

Ring's cover featured none other than Thomas Hearns, the WBA's new welterweight champion and Detroit's most popular boxer since Joe Louis.

Normally, a Ring cover of Hearns would have been welcomed at City Hall, which funded the amateur program that spawned him. But this wasn't a normal boxing spread.

Hearns was posed in a dark pinstripe suit and fedora, and he held an M-16 semi-automatic rifle. The headline read: "Detroit's "Hit Man" Takes Aim at Duran and Leonard."

The M-16 was a toy version purchased at a Manhattan department store, but that was not apparent to the naked eye. Hearns looked like he was armed and willing.

Young, elected in 1973 as one of the first black mayors of a major city, had labored mightily to repair Detroit's gang-infested and crime-ridden image, and now its newest celebrity was nicknamed "Hit Man."

Hearns' manager/trainer, Steward, was summoned to "discuss" the nickname. Steward often brought his top amateur fighters to meet Young and pose for photos. Young made his views clear to Steward, and overnight Hearns became the "Motor City Cobra." Or at least he tried to. But changing nicknames was like putting toothpaste back in the tube.

Problem was, "Hit Man" fit Hearns as comfortably as the tailored suits he wore. He had become "Hit Man" after he scored a 3rd-round knockout in a 1979 bout at Los Angeles. Expected at a post-fight party, Hearns told the limo driver to drop him at his hotel. A disappointed party guest summed up Hearns' aloofness, "He came in, did his job like a hit man, and left."

"Hit Man" tapped into his cold remorseless appearance – the flat expression and deep-set hooded eyes – but it missed his personality. Hearns had warmth usually hidden from public view. One Thanksgiving he visited a nursing home in New Orleans with Bob Arum's publicist Irving Rudd. He approached a startled 85-year-old resident and asked, "Can I have this dance with you?" Then he delicately twirled the delighted woman around the floor.

In front of media, however, he glowered on cue, and dutifully projected an air of menace. That was Hearns' intention moments after the "No Mas" bout, when he arrived at the Superdome media room where the press interviewed Leonard. He threw a rubber chicken at Leonard, and shouted "Chicken Ray."

He had reminded Leonard that they were both champions – supposedly equals. But it was an awkward stunt, and Leonard shrugged him off as if he were a pesky little brother.

Leonard's haughtiness was nothing new to Hearns. Leonard, two-and-a-half years older, was already an amateur star when Hearns started to make his name at Detroit's Kronk Recreation Center. Though Leonard's home gym was at Palmer Park, he was an icon at the Kronk, his photos plastered on the walls, and his career charted with obsessive interest.

"Ray was the first Kronk star," Steward recalled.

Hearns beat a path to Kronk in 1973, as a 14-year-old, on a crosstown bus. Kronk was on Detroit's west side, while Hearns lived on the gang-ridden east side, with his eight siblings and mother Lois, who worked as a clerk and a beautician. Hearns, the oldest boy, lived in the attic of their three-story house on Helen Street and plastered his walls with Elvis Presley posters, a vestige of his mother's Memphis roots. His sisters called him "Junior."

On Helen Street, Hearns excelled at the popular pastime of slap-boxing, and was in a gang called the Helen Hoods. Once, Hearns fell off a bike and broke his nose, incurring a sinus condition that would hamper his breathing and speech the rest of his life. But the injury did not stop him from slap-boxing or wanting to join the King Solomon boxing gym, which he did, at 10.

Hearns eventually was drawn to the Kronk, as were many youths of broken homes and poverty, because of Steward. He too had come from a broken home and poverty, and had won a national Golden Gloves title in 1963. When Hearns walked in Steward quickly sized him up. Hearns was like many of his young aspirants, fatherless and needing adult male guidance. Hearns, in fact, had never known his father. His surname had been taken from his stepfather, who barely merited mention in accounts of his youth. Steward became his surrogate father at the center of a Spartan cult of ring rats.

Kronk fighters engaged in fierce intramural battles and preferred sparring to bag and rope work. Fighters had to spar against larger fighters, often for longer than three minutes. If a fighter trained for a bout, Steward made him spar against a succession of fresh boxers, each instructed to go all out. Clinching was frowned upon as a mark of weakness.

With the basement gym stoked to a steamy 95 degrees, the army-green walls and asbestos-wrapped ceiling pipes pressed upon the practice ring in a stark simulation of a tropical boot camp. Only the toughest survived.

Steward gave Kronk fighters a technical approach typified by Hearns. They were taught to size up and adjust to an opponent – to box according to the situation. Combination punching and speed were requisites. A sturdy left jab was to stalk and set up a knockout punch.

Along with technical instruction, Steward gave them bright red-and-gold jackets with Kronk lettering across the back. Kronk's colors were as known throughout amateur boxing as the gold-and-blue of Notre Dame in college football. Long after he had become a world champion, Hearns wore his Kronk jacket. To him it was an identity.

Hearns won national Golden Gloves and AAU titles in 1977 and turned pro at 19. He was at his full height, 6-1, freakishly tall for a welterweight, with broad shoulders, a torso corded with hard muscle, taut waist, narrow hips, and flamingo-thin legs. His reach was 78½ inches, compared to Leonard's 74 and Hagler's 75.

His first pro bout was on the day after Thanksgiving, Nov. 25, 1977, at Detroit's old Olympia. Leonard, invited by Steward, was at ringside to see Hearns knock out Jerome Hill in two rounds.

After the fight Steward drove Leonard and Hearns to a small barbecue joint where they were photographed as they savored the ribs. At that moment, "Never in a million years did I think those two guys would fight each other," Steward recalled.

To return the favor Hearns agreed to help Leonard prepare for his next fight. Hearns traveled to Palmer Park and sparred with Leonard for the first time. The session started slowly and gradually escalated until it became an all-out exchange. Hearns got the better of it and slammed Leonard's headgear off kilter. Steward and Jacobs jumped in to stop it.

Nine months later Hearns was asked to help Leonard prepare for another bout. Jacobs opened his home to Hearns and welcomed him back to the gym. Once again Leonard and Hearns sparred, but this time they sniped at a distance, circled and darted. Later that evening Hearns phoned Steward.

"I did good," Hearns reported.

Jacobs told Steward that Hearns was "giving Ray the blues." Steward initially was surprised, and then – as if a light bulb went on – it dawned on him that Hearns and Leonard could well become opponents. He asked Jacobs to shut down their sparring and send Hearns back to Detroit.

In little over a year Hearns fought 14 times – all knockout victories within four rounds. By August 1980 Hearns had a record of 28-0. On August 2, 1980, Hearns knocked out Pipino Cuevas in the 2nd round to become the new WBA welterweight champion.

Not yet 22, Hearns bought himself a gold Cadillac and his mother a home in southwestern Detroit. He supported his 1-year-old son, Ronald, though he was too much of a ladies man to settle down. Still shy in a crowd, he felt increasingly comfortable at Las Vegas casinos, indulging a voracious appetite for gaming. He was meticulous about his body, abstained from liquor, drugs and pork, and maintained a rigorous conditioning regimen.

But something was missing. Hearns had two nicknames, a championship belt, and relative obscurity. It mattered little what the mayor of Detroit called him. To fans and media he was "the other welterweight champion" and would remain so until he beat Leonard.

Fortunately for Hearns, Leonard offered him a solution. Mike Trainer met separately with Steward and Hagler's attorney, Wainwright, in March 1981, as Leonard prepared to meet Larry Bonds (KO 10) in Syracuse. Hagler probably was used as a prop to gain leverage against Hearns, but when Hagler's managers demanded parity, and Steward did not, Leonard's choice was easy.

Their bout was set for September 16, 1981, at Las Vegas. Before they met, however, they took tune-up bouts, at the Houston Astrodome, in June 1981.

Hearns knocked out Pablo Baez, after which he joined a ringside TV crew to offer commentary on Leonard's bout against Ayub Kalule. Leonard spotted Hearns and shouted, "Shut up, you don't know how to talk anyway." Hearns, self-conscious about his mangled speech, was insulted. Leonard knocked out Kalule in the 9th round and won the WBA 154-pound title, which suggested that, when the time came, he could move up in weight for Hagler.

1981: Held by the Title

Seven months after Hagler became champion his mood had mellowed from anger to annoyance. He and Bertha had married and bought a house on Brockton's west side. He easily had won his first defense against a cartel-connected Venezuelan, Fulgencio Obelmejias, at Boston Garden. His purse had been $500,000, as it would be for his next defense, against Antuofermo.

On a balmy June afternoon he sat in an alcove of the Provincetown Inn. The championship had not turned out as expected, Hagler explained. If he held the title, he wondered, why did it feel as though it held him?

"I never worked so hard in my life," he said. "I've been really torn apart in a lot of ways, with my family, mother and father, aunts and uncles. Everybody wants a piece of you.

"Trying to do personal appearances, to get involved with endorsements, to control your own enterprise, trying to be a businessman, a family man, a father, taking care of ills, of the house…you can't neglect all these things.

"And you have to be here [training camp]. Mainly you know that this is what you have to do because you can't do it [box] forever.

"And then there's other people. Friends who say,

© Angie Carlino
Leonard's gig as an HBO commentator brought him to Brockton in 1981 to interview Hagler.

'Now you're champion and you don't have time for me.' Every five minutes somebody says to me, 'Marv, can you do this for me?' It only takes five minutes, and they think it's easy for you to do and it's not. Because I don't want to do anything I have to do. I want to do things I enjoy doing and that I do for people. That's the way I feel. I give up a lot of time. I figure that I'm very patient with people, but people also gotta be patient with me."

Hagler broke camp, he recounted, to be a guest in Brockton's centennial parade, and returned without visiting his family and home. Once back, he was asked to donate two fight tickets for a church raffle.

"I get mad sometimes 'cause I work so hard and people don't understand how hard I work," Hagler said. "I start bitchin' a little bit and my wife and mother say to me, 'Well, Marvin, this is what you wanted, isn't it?' And believe it or not, that calms me right down. I say, 'You're right, this is what I wanted.' So now I can start dealing with it again."

He was particularly bothered by an absence of endorsement and broadcasting opportunities.

"I feel I'm a more deserving person than what I've been getting," Hagler said. "Even with the money part, I feel I'm a million dollar fighter."

Asked if he measured his purses against Leonard's income, which was close to $20 million in 1980, Hagler nodded.

"Sure, I'd like to make his money," he said. "But I feel everything in time. If it's not there for you it's gonna come to you."

In June 1981 Hagler won a 4th-round TKO over Antuofermo. Three months later, in September, he was back in Provincetown to prepare for Mustafa Hamsho, a bout for which he was paid $1 million – the first time a middleweight reached the seven-figure plateau. He refused an invitation to attend the Leonard-Hearns bout because it would cost him three days of training. But he agreed to do a promotional spot for pay-per-view in the Boston area, and in it he beat the drums for his own big-money fight. "One of these guys will lose," he said. "The other one is doomed."

1981: "You're blowing it, son"

Leonard's left eye was a slit, and a few jabs more could close it. An angry bruise swelled under his right eye. As he slumped on his stool after the 12th round, Angelo Dundee worked on his battered face. Leonard suspected he was behind. Dundee, who had no doubt, invoked his inner Knute Rockne, and delivered a pep talk for the ages.

"Ray, you only got nine minutes left," Dundee shouted. "You're blowing it, son. You're blowing it now. Let's separate the men from the boys, now. Ray, you gotta fire – you're not firing. Ray, you're blowing it."

The bell rang for Round 13. An instant before Leonard arose, Dundee screamed into his right ear, "Speed!"

This was a bout that required no hype or promotion, got a lot, and lived up to it. It was the rare confluence of two brilliant young fighters in their early primes. The major difference was that Leonard was in his fourth Big Fight, while Hearns was in his first.

They fought behind Caesars, in a temporary outdoor stadium before 25,000-plus spectators, in temperatures that climbed above 100 under TV lights. Leonard made close to $9 million and Hearns close to $6 million with closed-circuit theater and pay-per-view TV revenues. The bout grossed a record $36 million. A promoter selected by Trainer, Dan Duva of Totowa, N.J., broke the Big Fight monopoly of King and Arum.

It was a rock opera of combat performed in five parts. In the first five rounds Leonard played possum as Hearns stalked. Hearns scored with long lefts, raised a knot under Leonard's left eye, and looked for an opening to unload a knockout punch. Leonard boxed at a distance and appeared unable to solve Hearns' long arms and slashing punches.

In the 6th round Leonard sprang his trap. He stepped forward, surprised Hearns, and landed a crushing left to the jaw. Hearns was staggered and nearly went down. Leonard sustained his onslaught throughout the 6th and into the 7th, when again it appeared Hearns was on the verge of going down. But Leonard's ambush did not anticipate Hearns' reservoir of grit nor his ring general-ship – all of which he drew upon to survive.

Now Leonard was spent, and worse, his left eye was swollen halfway shut. But the roles were reversed, Leon-ard stalked Hearns and Hearns circled and flicked jabs from a distance. In rounds 9 though 12 Hearns continued his movement and gradually regained his command and confidence. In the 12th Hearns backed Leonard up with a left hook–right uppercut combination and once again was the aggressor.

When Dundee exhorted Leonard after the 12th, neither of them knew that Hearns, who had never fought more than 12 rounds and who had dried out more than necessary to make weight, was virtually depleted. The heat and pace had sapped his matchstick legs.

A minute into the 13th round Leonard resumed the furious attack that had marked the 6th and 7th rounds. He scored with an overhand right, then a left, as Hearns backpedaled and slipped to the canvas. Leonard unleashed a windmill that Hearns, unschooled in the art of the clinch, was unable to smother. Hearns wobbled, was pounded into the ropes, and fell through, though it was ruled a push. He climbed to his feet, was barraged once again, and went down near the same spot. Hearns took a standing nine count and was saved by the bell.

Leonard instantly attacked in the 14th. Hearns covered up in vain as Leonard flurried and snapped back his head with short uppercuts. After 20 or 30 unanswered punches, as Leonard signaled with his right hand to referee Dave Pearl for a stoppage, Pearl stepped in.

When it was stopped, Hearns was ahead by 4 points, 3 points, and 2 points on the scorecards, which surprised Leonard and media and touched off criticism of the 10-point system.

The next day Leonard appeared before media, with his swollen eyes hidden behind sunglasses, and was asked if he planned to fight Hagler. His coy response suggested he was in no hurry to do so.

"I feel the longer I wait the older Hagler gets," Leonard said.

CHAPTER 8

· · · · · · · · · · · · · · · · · · · ·

1982: Legally Marvelous

WILLIAM "CAVEMAN" LEE CHALLENGED Hagler in March 1982. Hagler asked ABC to identify him on-air as "Marvelous Marvin Hagler," but the network refused, even though it saw fit to use Lee's nickname. Hagler was infuriated, and after he knocked out Lee in the 1st round, he petitioned Plymouth County Probate Court to change his name to "Marvelous Marvin."

The court required Hagler to produce his birth certificate from the City of Newark, thus confirming his birth date of May 23, 1954. Before the petition was approved Wainwright explained to Hagler that his true age would be made public. "He hesitated momentarily, and decided to go through with it," Wainwright recalled. Though his last name legally was now "Marvin," public, press, and Hagler himself continued to use "Hagler" as a last name. Nor did "Marvelous" catch on as a first name – he was still "Marvin" to family, friends, fans, and media.

Bertha gave birth to a girl, Charelle, early in 1982, as Hagler, the Petronellis, and Arum maneuvered to find him a bout appropriate for his new name. They settled on Hearns, ostensibly as an elimination bout for the right to meet Leonard. After Leonard's surgery in May the proposed Hagler-Hearns bout, never on sound financial footing, fell apart. Hagler's handlers blamed Hearns when they should have looked in a mirror.

At this point Hagler's sense of victimization was justified – he was the victim of flawed management. The Petronelli brothers and Arum had tied him to a second multi-bout deal with HBO, the young pay-cable channel, which limited his maneuverability. His handlers had allowed the sanctioning bodies to rule his selection of opponents, when he should have ignored them, as Leonard had. Nonetheless, Hagler remained steadfastly loyal to the two brothers from Brockton.

In July Hagler suffered a cracked rib while training for another $500,000 defense against Obelmejias. The next morning he winced while settling onto a couch in the lobby of the Provincetown Inn. The pain in his rib equaled the dejection on his face.

"They tell you when you're the best money is gonna come," Hagler said. "Well, I been hangin' in there. They say when you're champion people will come to you with their products. This stuff is supposed to happen, but it hasn't for Marvin Hagler. It's been kinda slow.

"I'm a million dollar fighter. I feel cheated getting $500,000."

As Hagler shifted on the couch, his cracked rib sent another knife-like reminder of his aggrieved situation.

"What else can happen to me?" Hagler asked.

On November 9 Hagler had the answer. He flew to Baltimore, and expected Leonard to make him $10 million wealthier. Instead, he watched Leonard announce his retirement.

He was Marvelous, but his career was not.

1982: R.I.P. Duk-Koo Kim

Four nights after Leonard's retirement announcement in Baltimore, he was reminded, tragically, of the peril he no longer faced.

Leonard was with CBS in Las Vegas for the bout between 135-pound champion Ray "Boom Boom" Mancini and challenger Duk-Koo Kim, the son of a Korean rice farmer. The night before the bout Kim, 23, had scribbled in his hotel room, "Kill or be killed."

Leonard witnessed a bruising match, waged evenly for 7 rounds, between two fighters with similar head-to-head styles. From the 8th round on Mancini gained the upper hand, and by the 12th Kim stumbled and took unanswered punches to the head. Mancini unleashed a thunderous barrage in the 13th, and landed forty unanswered punches, mostly to the head. Kim appeared defenseless, but somehow mounted an attack late in the round that kept the bout from being stopped. Mancini finally decked Kim with a hard right in the 14th round to end the bout. Kim was helped to his corner, where he slumped over and fell into a coma. Four days later he died. His devastated mother later committed suicide, and Kim became a cult hero in Korea, celebrated in a film, *Champion*.

Kim's death, nearly three years after Willie Classen's death, spurred urgent calls for reform. By the end of 1982 one of the governing bodies, the World Boxing Council, eliminated the 15-round championship distance in favor of 12 rounds. Early in 1983 the *Journal of the American Medical Association* called for a ban on boxing, and short of that, empowerment of ringside doctors to stop a fight at any time.

Yet another ghost whispered to Leonard. In retirement he was safe from subdural hematoma, coma, and the indignity of punch drunkenness. His abdication had deflated Hagler, but left him, at 26, with his eyesight, health, money in the bank, broadcasting career, adoring public, and a loving family. Leonard's life seemed almost too good to be true. And so it was.

CHAPTER 9

· · · · · · · · · · · · · · · · · · · ·

1983: Cocaine

WITHOUT AN OPPONENT TO fool, Leonard fooled himself. He descended into a demimonde of entertainers and celebrities where cocaine was as routine as first-class travel, four-star hotels and restaurants, VIP rooms, red carpets, and thick rolls of cash. His lifestyle damaged his health, destroyed his marriage, and alienated his children and parents.

"I'd go to parties, take a leak, and there was cocaine right there," Leonard recounted years later.

Typical of Leonard's schedule was an event shortly after his "retirement" announcement. The NAACP 15th annual Image Awards Ceremony took place at the Hollywood Palladium on Dec. 6, 1982. Thirty black actors, musicians, and sports figures were honored for presenting positive images of blacks. Leonard, Magic Johnson, Rod Carew, and Franco Harris were the four athletes honored.

Singer Lena Horne, actresses Jayne Kennedy, Cecily Tyson, Marla Gibbs, actors Lou Gossett Jr., Moses Gunn, Paul Winfield, and Sherman Hemsley, and musicians BB King, Al Jarreau, and Kool & The Gang won awards. Kennedy, the beautiful actress–TV sports reporter, was linked with Leonard in gossip.

Los Angeles was now his favorite environ. His celebrity friends included Richard Pryor, Michael and Jermaine Jackson, LeVar Burton, Ben Vereen, Lola Falana, Natalie Cole, Barry White, Whoopi Goldberg, Michael J. Fox, and even an aged comedian, Milton Berle.

Pryor, a boxing fan, had suffered third-degree burns over half his body in June 1980 as he free-based cocaine. In the hospital, he

© Ollie Dunlap
Singer Natalie Cole and Sugar Ray Leonard.

used a new technology, pay-per-view TV, to watch the first Leonard-Duran match. Pryor met Leonard through James Anderson, the burly bodyguard who lived in Los Angeles and had developed, through his association with Ali, a large celebrity clientele. Anderson often accompanied Leonard on his nocturnal romps.

"If socially there happened to be a young lady Ray took a fancy to and she was going to go with us, James was pretty good at screening," said Ollie Dunlap. "There

© Ollie Dunlap

Advisor Ollie Dunlap, left, dancer Lola
Falana, and Sugar Ray Leonard.

might be 60 girls in a club, but 40 came every weekend. James knew who the party girls were and who were there to get drinks."

Meanwhile, Leonard's well-paid jobs as ringside commentator for HBO and CBS kept him on the road, often in Las Vegas, where women and drugs were virtual tourist attractions. As his dissipation gathered momentum friends and associates began to notice. Gil Clancy, the veteran CBS boxing commentator, was among the first to notice Leonard's frequent trips to airplane lavatories, and the telltale signs around his nose. One morning at his Las Vegas hotel suite, Leonard was found seated on the edge of his bed by his brother, Roger, and Dunlap. "I got ripped off," he told them, sheepishly. A woman had stolen his jewelry and cash. He had slept through her stealthy departure after a night of drugs and sex.

"That was the last time we let girls into Ray's room," Dunlap said. "He would use my room and I would sleep in his."

When Leonard turned to cocaine – in 1983 according to his own recollection – he was late to the party, or debacle, such as it was. America's elite athletes, entertainers, and musicians acquired the habit throughout the 1970s, lulled by popular culture and mass media into thinking it fashionable and benign. A 1977 *Newsweek* story reported, "Among hostesses in the smart sets of Los Angeles and New York, a little cocaine, like Dom Perignon and Beluga caviar, is now de rigueur at dinners. Some party givers pass it around with the canapés on silver trays...the user experiences a feeling of potency, of confidence, of energy."

The new decade was two days old when Bernard King of the Utah Jazz was arrested in Salt Lake City and charged with sodomy, forcible sexual abuse, and possession of cocaine. Another Jazz player, Terry Furlow, died in May 1980 after crashing his car at 4 a.m. in a Cleveland suburb with traces of cocaine in his system. A *Los Angeles Times* article in August 1980 asserted that 40 to 75 percent of NBA players used cocaine, based on estimates of players and executives.

Cocaine allegations engulfed Duran after the "No Mas" bout, supposedly because he had resorted to cocaine, an appetite suppressant, to shed more than 30 pounds. Duran denied it and his manager, Carlos Eleta, professed not to know. In the late 1980s Eleta would be jailed in Georgia and charged with smuggling cocaine.

A *Time* magazine article in 1981 showed a champagne glass full of sparkling white powder with the headline "High on Cocaine – a Drug with Status and Menace." Former Minnesota Vikings All-Pro Carl Eller went public with his cocaine habit in September 1981, saying it had cost him $2000 a week, wrecked his personal life, and eroded his football skills before he underwent treatment.

Leonard's eye surgery preceded by a month a shocking exposé in *Sports Illustrated* magazine. In June 1982 a former New Orleans Saints lineman, Don Reese, who had been convicted of selling cocaine in 1977, co-authored a cover story that alleged widespread drug abuse in the NFL. Reese, who played for the Saints from 1978 to 1980, claimed that players snorted coke in the locker room before games and at halftime "and stayed up all hours of the night roaming the streets to get more stuff." Cocaine use in the NFL was so extensive, Reese wrote, that it "now controls and corrupts the game."

Shortly thereafter the Saints top running back and former Heisman Trophy winner, George Rogers, told a federal grand jury in New Orleans that he had spent $10,000 on cocaine since joining the league in 1981. Saints running back Chuck Muncie told a New Orleans newspaper that he had bought cocaine from former Saints running back Michael Strachan, who was under indictment for distribution.

In the summer of 1982 the Justice Department began a drug probe on Capitol Hill that targeted congressmen and top aides. It would last 18 months and cost the government $2 million before it quietly fizzled, with only the convictions of six tour guides and elevator operators.

After the 1982 baseball season Montreal Expos outfielder Tim Raines checked into a 30-day detox program at a California treatment center. After completing it, Raines confessed publicly that he had spent $40,000 on cocaine in the first nine months of 1982, and that he had snorted between innings in the bathroom behind the dugout, and before games in the parking lot outside the stadium. Raines had hidden little gram bottles of cocaine in his batting glove or pocket, and when he carried the bottles in his pocket he would be sure to slide into a base head first, to protect his investment,

By 1983 executives in the NFL, NBA, and Major League Baseball routinely inquired about potential "chemical imbalance" before they obtained a player. Dodgers reliever Steve Howe became the first known "second-offender" in any major sport, and four Kansas City Royals – former Cy Young winner Vida Blue, Willie Wilson, Willie Mays Aikens, and Jerry Martin – were sentenced to three months in prison for cocaine possession.

Leonard turned to cocaine, he later claimed, after his eye injury drove him from the ring. As Rick Reilly wrote in *Sports Illustrated*, Leonard had left the ring "for a world of HBO stand-ups and life as a human cummerbund." Most elite athletes disengage gradually. With Leonard it happened virtually overnight, at a relatively young age, 26, and left a vacuum. He claimed that cocaine and alcohol helped him cope with what he described as depression.

"I used it when I felt bad...when I missed competing...during periods of great depression," Leonard said.

Juanita also believed depression was a factor in Leonard's use of cocaine and alcohol.

"Commentating just was not enough," Juanita recounted. "He was the kind of fighter that did it, and that being taken away from him, I think devastated him more than any negative event in his life."

1983: "You beat him"

Hagler loaded his family into a 36-foot recreational vehicle and drove west in late summer of 1983. Escorted in a separate car by photographer Angie Carlino and a friend, Jack Hurley, Hagler covered 36 states and 11,000 miles, staying at KOA campgrounds, with stops at Mt. Rushmore and at a dude ranch in Wyoming. Hagler rode horses and ate exotic foods such as alligator and buffalo steak.

By now, Hagler knew to trade his celebrity for drinks, meals, accommodations, and souvenirs. "He learned how to play," Carlino recalled. Though comfortably wealthy, Hagler's frugality was deeply ingrained. He complained that disclosure of his purses set him up as a mark for scams, and asked Arum to keep the figures private. He kept a short rein on Brockton accountant Peter Mareb, who handled his finances. Hagler met once a month with Mareb and was active in investment decisions. He insisted on a conservative portfolio heavy on bonds, which stood him in good stead when the stock market nosedived in 1987. To Arum, Hagler had become a "classic New England Yankee" who lived below his means and abjured ostentation. In this, Hagler channeled Marciano, a legendary penny-pincher, but was distinct from many free-spending champions who had come to financial ruin.

In small towns Hagler stopped at local gyms and chatted with fighters. Everywhere, admirers lavished him with warmth and respect. In Hollywood Hagler was a guest on the sets of two TV shows, "M*A*S*H" and "Dynasty," and one film, *Johnny Dangerously*. The making of entertainment fascinated Hagler; he sat for hours watching the oft-tedious work and never seemed bored or impatient. To actress Joan Collins, the star of "Dynasty," he offered a Marvelous Marvin t-shirt. She graciously accepted but declined to wear it.

If Hagler was in an unusually good mood on vacation there was a reason. A multi-million dollar payday had materialized with the most unexpected opponent – Roberto Duran. A little more than 2½ years after his "No Mas" disgrace, Duran had climbed off the scrap heap and won a junior middleweight title. When Duran knocked out Davey Moore in 8 rounds, in June 1983, among the audience at Madison Square Garden were Hagler and his oldest son, Gentry. Duran's resurrection occurred shortly after Hagler, bored by his recent opponents (Tony Sibson, TKO 6; Wilford Scypion, KO 4) and worn down by his harsh training regimen, had hinted at retirement. "How long can you keep beating your head against a wall?" Hagler asked. "How long can you keep psyching yourself? How long can you keep getting your body in shape?"

Now thoughts of retirement receded as an ebullient Hagler told reporters, "I would like to have seen (Duran) get out of the game, but I guess this proves that if you hang around long enough you get what's coming to you." Arum immediately declared a Hagler-Duran bout to be "the fight everyone wants to see" and pegged Hagler's purse at $5 million plus a percentage of the closed-circuit revenues. By the time Hagler finished his vacation 2½ months later the bout was set.

The bout, on November 10, 1983, at Caesars Pal-

© Angie Carlino

Roberto Duran, left, and Marvelous Marvin Hagler
before their 1983 bout at Caesars Palace.

ace, was Hagler's first Big Fight, namely, one that tran-
scended boxing and captured a general sports audience.
The best part of it, from Hagler's perspective, was that
he was a supporting character to Duran's lead. The marketing hook was Duran's bid to redeem himself after
the humiliation of No Mas. "The glory, the fall, and the
redemption," was how Luis Spada, Duran's new trainer-
manager, described it.

The worst part of it, from Hagler's perspective, was
that he respected and liked Duran. Hagler had been a fan
of Duran's, and had watched his bouts on TV, throughout
the 1970s. Just a few months earlier Hagler and Duran had
been guests of comedian Bob Hope on a TV special. The

two had warmed to one another, though Hagler backed off when he sensed Duran had sized him up for the ring.

Duran was long past being the best pound-for-pound boxer he had been a decade earlier at 135 pounds. At 156½ pounds he no longer was as fast, and his punch did not numb larger opponents. But he still was clever, and experienced, and he understood the Fight Game as well as anybody. He knew, for instance, that Hagler was conflicted, unable to objectify him, as he had other opponents. Indeed, at the New York press conference announcing the bout, Duran held out his hand, and after a brief hesitation, Hagler shook it – perhaps the only time in his career he shook an opponent's hand before a bout.

Leonard, for HBO, covered a press conference attended by both fighters two days before the bout. Arum, the promoter, accorded Leonard a tongue-in-cheek acknowledgment.

"Guys who are contenders start hanging around, and this guy really wants to fight the winner," Arum said. "He's a contender…a fairly decent fighter…Sugar Ray Leonard."

Leonard smiled good-naturedly, palms up in surrender. His reaction was not persuasive. Later that day, he told *Post* columnist Dave Kindred that he had no intention of fighting again. In the next breath, however, he said that life was "unpredictable" and that he missed the challenge, the competition, and "the threat" of boxing.

Though a 4-1 favorite, Hagler nearly lost the fight. Duran chose to box, feint, move at angles, and induce Hagler to miss. Hagler fought without urgency or fire, and repeatedly walked into Duran's sneaky right hand counter. When Hagler hurt Duran in the 6th round, inexplicably, he failed to follow up.

Though a difficult bout to score, after 13 rounds two judges had Duran ahead by one point and the third judge had it even. Hagler won the last two rounds, solidly, to salvage an uninspired performance. At the final bell, Duran leaned through the ropes, and said to Leonard, "You beat him."

Leonard turned to Dunlap and said, "He picks up his foot first – I can tap him every time he picks it up."

Sour reviews preceded an angry accounting of revenues. Bill Nack, in *Sports Illustrated*, wrote of Hagler, "He's a stalker, conservative and cautious, almost insecure, whose ring presence can be likened to that of a mechanic in a garage – speak softly and carry a big wrench."

Hagler expected to bank his $5 million guarantee plus a percentage of closed-circuit TV revenues, but he was infuriated to learn that his "upside" never kicked in despite a $30 million gross. Wainwright, the Brockton attorney who had pulled political strings to advance Hagler's career, was blamed and fired.

Three months later Leonard invited HBO broadcaster Barry Tompkins, in Miami for a telecast, to lunch on a chartered boat. As they sat on the bow, Leonard brought up Hagler.

"He said, 'You want to know how to beat Marvin Hagler?'" Tompkins recalled. "'I'll tell you how. You've got to fight for 10 seconds, or 15 seconds, three times every round, and the last 15 seconds, particularly. That's how you beat Marvin Hagler.'"

CHAPTER 10

. . . .

1984: Down the Toilet

ONE NIGHT, IN THE latter half of 1984, Leonard returned to his turreted stone mansion in an agitated state. At a glance Juanita saw that he was strung out, and erratic. She watched him rummage through a drawer, then wheel on her.

"Where is it?"

"Down the toilet. Where it belongs."

In a fury, he pulled Juanita from their bed, slapped her, and flung her like a rag doll across the spacious master bedroom. She tumbled across the floor and rolled up against a chest of drawers, ears ringing, half-dazed. Juanita slowly rose to her feet and gathered her dignity as Leonard screamed profanities and waved his gun in the air.

"I'm going to kill myself," he said.

She stared.

"You don't believe me, do you?"

Juanita did not reply. She knew that whatever she said he would turn it against her. But her silence was inflammatory, too, in his deranged state. He threw a lamp against the wall, smashing it into tiny pieces of metal and wood. Now his bloodshot eyes glowed a demonic hue. He kicked a mirror and watched its jagged shards drop onto the carpet.

She tried to walk away, to get out of the bedroom, but he stalked her with mounting rage. She turned to face him just in time to see his fist whistling through the air, just in time to duck. The blow glanced against her forehead, and his ring opened a cut. As she felt the damp warm blood with her fingers, Juanita drew herself up and calmly walked out of the bedroom. Leonard, suddenly overcome with horror and shame, trailed behind.

"I'm sorry," he shouted. "Please."

She knew what she had to do. She pulled the two terrified boys from their bedrooms, carrying the baby, and hurried toward the front door. She intended to leave – and never come back. But when they scuttled across the gleaming front foyer she saw he had gotten there first – blocking the door. The gun was gone. Now Leonard held a can of kerosene.

"We're leaving."

"No."

"We're leaving. I'm afraid of you."

Leonard lifted up the can, unscrewed the cap and matter-of-factly poured kerosene on the wooden floor.

"If you leave," he said, "I'll burn this house down before I let you get it. Or anything else in it."

Juanita stiffened. He wasn't holding a match – not yet, anyway. No time for negotiating. No time for good-byes. She shielded Little Ray with her body, and pushed him out the front door. Cradling the baby, she followed into the brisk night air, and as she fingered her car keys, Leonard ranted in the foyer.

Leonard's cocaine habit and domestic violence, as described in Juanita's divorce deposition in 1990, reached their apex in the year after the Hagler-Duran bout.

Though Juanita testified that it occurred as late as 1987, Leonard said he used cocaine only between 1983 and 1986, and associates said it became most problematic late in 1984.

After the bout, in late 1983, Leonard had returned to the gym. He ran and exercised, and every two or three days he jumped rope and hit the bags. "I've been drinking and need to sweat it off," he told associates.

But there was more to it. The longer Leonard was out of the ring the more his celebrity dimmed. He still worked as a commentator and had a few endorsements, and he was in a commercial with Little Ray for a hot cocoa mix, but in general, ovations were quieter and autograph requests fewer. To Leonard, the relative silence was deafening.

"It was cruel and unusual punishment," *Los Angeles Times* columnist Jim Murray wrote later. "He had to sit there and ooh and aah and gush and exclaim over a fighter he knew wouldn't give him much more trouble than a heavy bag or his shadow."

The antidote, Leonard concluded, was a comeback.

"The man inside of me is saying: 'I have to come out,'" Leonard explained. His alter ego, Sugar Ray, had spoken.

Assured by physicians that his surgically repaired left eye was sound, he chose as an opponent journeyman Kevin Howard, whose record was 20-4-1. Leonard-Howard took place on May 11, 1984, in Worcester, Mass. The choice of location, in Hagler's backyard, foreshadowed Leonard's obvious intention. Hagler, who had knocked out Juan Roldán in March, was at ringside with his wife, Bertha. Tentative plans for a bout, worth $10 million to each fighter, were to be announced the following day. Hagler told a reporter, "If he's foolish enough to step in the ring with me, I'm foolish enough to rip his eye out."

But Leonard had underestimated his physical attrition. Though he had gone "clean" to prepare for Howard, his body was thin and relatively frail at 149 pounds. Shockingly, in the 4th round a straight right by Howard sent Leonard to the canvas for the first time in his pro career. His face registered indignation as he clambered to his feet. He continued, though every round was a struggle and he was in pain. Leonard managed to stop Howard in the 9th round.

Minutes later, in the dressing room, he asked himself, "If this guy can do this to me, what could Hagler do?"

Then he told Juanita, who was eight months' pregnant, "This is it, I'm giving it up."

"You can't retire," Juanita said. "People will think Kevin Howard made you retire."

"Sweetheart, he did."

To the media Leonard said, "There's no sense trying

to fool myself or anyone else – I just don't have it anymore," he said.

Word of Leonard's decision reached Hagler at ringside as he watched another fight. "It's the story of my life," Hagler said.

Leonard soon fell back into his self-destructive habits. The birth of his second son, Jarrel, in June barely interrupted his routine, and his mood gradually became uneven and volatile, according to Juanita's testimony. Some days were better than others. On the good days Leonard got high, shot pool with his buddies, usually Joe Broddie and Julius "Juice" Gatling, and spent the night with a girlfriend. Juanita had long ago accepted his infidelity as an occupational hazard. When Leonard stayed out, at least she and the children were out of the line of fire.

On the bad days, Juanita feared for herself, Little Ray, and the baby.

Juanita later said that while she received counseling during this period, Leonard refused it.

"He was in denial – he didn't think he had a problem," Juanita recounted. "He didn't think it was a problem in doing drugs and alcohol, and the drugs and alcohol turned him into a person that he really wasn't. It turned him into a kind of a monster."

Years later, Leonard blamed his behavior on his hangers-on.

"My wife said, 'The drugs are killing you, you shouldn't hang with those guys.' But then I'd be with my guys, so who do you listen to, the guys or your wife? I listened to the guys."

Leonard's problems were largely concealed from *Washington Post* reporter William Gildea in March 1985, when Gildea visited Leonard's Potomac mansion. Gildea's feature for the *Post*'s Sunday magazine depicted domestic serenity and marital harmony, with Leonard and Juanita describing one another as "best friends." Leonard told Gildea he had accepted his retirement and had no urge to fight again.

"I could sense this palpable emptiness in his life at the time I wrote that piece," Gildea recalled. "He hadn't done what he wanted to do."

1984: Two Locomotives – One Track

Hagler knocked out Mustafa Hamsho in three rounds at Madison Square Garden in October 1984. When it ended, Thomas Hearns climbed into the ring. As the Hagler family, seated at ringside, chanted, "We want Hearns, we want Hearns," he smiled and beckoned the clan to chant louder.

Hagler's relatives weren't the only ones. More than 16,000 had come to the Garden, not because they expected much from Hamsho, but because they could see Hagler and Hearns converge like two locomotives from opposite ends of the same track.

After Leonard's fourth retirement, the largest payday available to Hagler and Hearns was each other. Since his loss to Leonard, Hearns had captured a 154-pound title and won eight straight, including a devastating 2nd-round knockout of Duran in June.

© Angie Carlino

Thomas Hearns wearing his WBC 154-pound championship belt, early 1985.

Hagler beat the drums with classic victim-speak. "I missed my glory when I won my title in London," he said. "I thought I could get it with Leonard. Now I hope it will come with Hearns."

Hagler-Hearns was made for April 15, 1985, to be held in the parking lot stadium behind Caesars. Hagler was guaranteed $5.3 million, and Hearns $5.2 million, with additional closed-circuit theater percentages. The only hurdle had been the number of rounds. Hearns, who had wilted after the 12th in his loss to Leonard, insisted on 12 rounds. Hagler resisted, but gave in, convinced that Hearns would walk away otherwise. It was a concession Leonard would remember, two years hence.

Hagler and Hearns got on one another's nerves, in near-comical fashion, long before they climbed into the ring. In February 1985, the two fighters, in separate private jets, embarked on a 21-city 12-day promotional tour that included two press conferences a day, and a cocktail party at night. Hearns complained that Hagler's jet had an electronic "Pac-Man" game while his did not, and that Hagler wasn't spending enough time at the cocktail parties for high-rolling customers of Caesars Palace. Hagler

© Angie Carlino

Thomas Hearns, left, and Marvelous Marvin
Hagler, before their 1985 bout.

complained that Hearns had commandeered a limousine
that was supposed to be his, and that Hearns was stealing
his best lines at press conferences. When Hagler voiced
impatience with the tour, Hearns pulled him aside and
said, "What's wrong with you, man? We've got to do this
to sell the fight. We're putting money in our pockets."
Hagler replied, "Don't worry about me – worry about
yourself."

One day they found themselves in Leonard's old gym
in Palmer Park, Md., filming a TV spot for the Internal

Revenue Service. Arum's publicist, Irving Rudd, conceived of the spot, wherein both fighters said they filed their tax returns early because they would be busy on filing day – April 15. The ad reached a universal audience and helped ratchet up sales.

The fight had no clear favorite, and bets poured in equally on both. What ultimately sold it was the anticipation of a nasty rumble between two fighters with axes to grind. Both had been teased and used by Leonard, had toiled in his shadow, and felt unappreciated. Now it was time to stake out their legacies. Hagler and Hearns were ready to make a dramatic and violent statement.

CHAPTER 11

· ·

1985: A Black Christ

THE STARK FINAL IMAGE was that of Hearns, "now helpless, semiconscious, looking very like a black Christ taken from the cross," in the arms of a solemn aide.

The scene was "powerful, haunting, unsettling...cruelly beautiful," wrote essayist and novelist Joyce Carol Oates.

Hagler and Hearns fought as if possessed in the parking lot behind Caesars. Hagler's pent-up bitterness found release in a violent attack, even as each crack of Hearns' gloves reinforced a lifetime of slights. In the end, Hearns was martyred to absolve Hagler of victimization.

The 1st round is legendary, among the most vicious and splendid ever fought on the Big Fight stage. Action accelerated so recklessly that spectators were left breathless. Punches windmilled into a blur, though the actual count was 82 punches for Hagler and 83 for Hearns, about three times that of a typical round. Hagler did not throw a single jab. During one of the toe-to-toe exchanges a cut was opened on Hagler's forehead above his right eye and blood began to flow. And in the final minute Hearns' right hand cracked against Hagler's skull and fractured. Indeed, Hagler seemed intent on proving the adage that a good chin will beat a good punch. Two judges scored the round for Hagler, one for Hearns.

The pace in the second was only slightly less furious, though Hearns now was limited with his right hand. Hagler maintained his attack, confused Hearns while switching between southpaw and orthodox stances, and gradually asserted control. By the third minute Hearns was off balance and his legs were shaky.

Early in the 3rd round Hagler appeared on the verge of closing out Hearns when, suddenly, the bout was almost snatched from him. His cut re-opened and a torrent of blood ran over his nose. Referee Richard Steele halted the action and escorted Hagler to his corner. Hagler felt a conspiracy coming on, another plot to hold him down. "I will not let you stop this fight," he told Steele. He later admitted to thinking, "Why were they doing this to me?"

The ringside physician examined the cut and deemed Hagler able to continue. Steele asked him if he was able to see. "I'm not missing him, am I?" Hagler snapped. Steele had to agree.

When the fight resumed Hagler attacked quickly to end it. He bounced three long rights off Hearns' head, the last one twisting him downward, as one writer put it, "like a beach umbrella caught in the wind." Hearns struggled to his feet but Steele wrapped him up and stopped the bout. A moment later Hearns sagged into the arms of an aide with whom he was joined in the photograph that stole the breath of Oates and the public.

Mobbed in the ring, Hagler was handed his 3-year-old daughter, Charelle, by Bertha. "Hi baby," he said. The toddler looked at his cut forehead and said, "Boo boo."

HBO's Larry Merchant crowded Hagler with a microphone and quickly found out what was on Hagler's mind. "I told you a long time ago I was a great fighter, and you said 'you still have to prove yourself,'" Hagler said. "Well, did I do that tonight?" Minutes later Hagler appeared before the assembled media and said, "Maybe now I'll get some commercials."

Meanwhile, Leonard, part of the HBO crew, had picked up another tic in Hagler's style. "I think I can beat him," he told Dunlap.

Later, in a dressing room, as Hagler slipped into the coat of an expensive suit, he was congratulated by Duane Ford, the chairman of the Nevada Athletic Commission.

"Marvin, you look like a million bucks," Ford said.

Hagler tightened his tie and appraised himself in a mirror.

"Make that six million, Mr. Ford."

In actuality, Hagler's purse reached $8 million. Brockton honored him again outside of City Hall though now his profile was national. He appeared on Johnny Carson's "Tonight" Show and "Saturday Night Live," made TV commercials for a deodorant and a pizza chain, and, with his wife and family, visited President Reagan at the White House.

But the most relevant moment occurred just five days later, when HBO shot a post-fight show, with Leonard and Tompkins as hosts. Leonard and Tompkins were in a New York studio, and Hearns, his right hand in a cast, was in a Detroit studio. Hagler was supposed to be in a Boston studio, but he was late. The bright lights and cameras were on, though shooting had not begun. Leonard and Hearns could see one another on monitors, and for an hour they chatted. Finally, Hagler, his forehead bandaged, arrived and joined the other two on camera.

"Hey, Marvin," Leonard said. "You want to buy a Ferrari?"

"What color is it?"

"Red."

"I'll tell you, Ray," Hagler said. "They stop a lot of red cars up here in Massachusetts."

At this, Hearns chuckled.

"Hey, Ray, your Ferrari there must really be a lemon," he said. "You been trying to sell it for an hour."

Hearns' message to Hagler was clear. Don't buy a used car from Sugar Ray Leonard.

1985: Nose to Nose

Now at the pinnacle, Hagler succumbed to temptation, as Leonard had. He drifted away from Bertha and their children, took an apartment in Boston, cavorted with women and allegedly found cocaine.

Most of what is known about Hagler's cocaine use was alleged and reported by John Dennis, a Boston TV and radio personality. Dennis did not report on Hagler's cocaine dissipation until 1987, after he fought Leonard, though he claims he was aware of it by the latter part of 1985. Hagler denied that he used cocaine but chose not to press a legal challenge to Dennis' 1987 report.

"My understanding from the Petronellis was that Marvin began to use cocaine extensively after the Hearns fight," said Dennis, then the sports anchor for Channel 7 in Boston. (In public comments and to this author, Pat Petronelli denied that he provided information to Dennis, and denied that Hagler used cocaine.)

Independent of the Petronellis, a Brockton cop and a bartender at Logan Airport tipped Dennis to Hagler's cocaine use.

"The cop said 'tell your boxing buddy to send a stooge to the crack house. How smart is it to drive a Caddy with MMH license plates to the house of a known drug dealer, park in front, and come out five minutes later? Tell him to smarten the fuck up,'" recalled Dennis.

"The bartender said he couldn't count the number of times he saw Marvin chasing his nose all over town – night after night."

Photographer Angie Carlino, who had accompanied Hagler on his cross-country vacation in 1983, dated Hagler's cocaine use to this period. Hagler had distanced himself because Carlino did not use cocaine and had stopped drinking.

"The DEA had tapes of him coming out of crack joints," Carlino recalled. "They would pull him out of his car. Bertha would come get him."

Betty Whitney, Pat Petronelli's wife-to-be, said she had no first-hand knowledge of Hagler using cocaine. "But it's hard to imagine that stuff wasn't pushed on him by the celebrities he was around," Whitney said.

Hagler was supposed to fight a little-known and undefeated Ugandan, John "The Beast" Mugabi, in November, but he had lost focus and drive. In late October he claimed a sore back and asked that the bout be postponed. Arum complained that a sore back wasn't reason enough, at which point Hagler claimed a broken nose. The bout was rescheduled for March.

The drumbeat of cocaine-related scandal grew louder. The Pittsburgh cocaine trial, in September 1985, implicated 19 major league players, including two former MVPs, Keith Hernandez and Dave Parker, who testified as government witnesses. Hernandez, in his testimony, called cocaine "the demon in me" and "the devil on this earth." Parker testified that his primary supplier had had access to the Pittsburgh Pirates clubhouse. None of the players were defendants, but their testimony helped convict Philadelphia caterer-cum-dealer Curtis Strong, who was sentenced to 12 years.

Chuck Wepner, a Bayonne, N.J., liquor salesman, was arrested in November and charged with being a "mid-level" cocaine dealer. Wepner, known as the "Bayonne Bleeder," had knocked down Ali before being stopped in the 15th round of their 1975 title fight, and had been Sylvestor Stallone's model for the film character, "Rocky." The same month Kansas City Chiefs defensive end Mike Bell and twin brother Mark, a former NFL player, were arrested in Wichita and charged with distribution of cocaine.

In December 1985 news reports indicated that five of the St. Louis Cardinals (NFL) had used cocaine during the last two seasons. In New Orleans, local gambler Gary Kranz was sentenced for his role in a point-shaving scandal involving the Tulane University basketball team. Kranz had obtained cocaine for several players as part of his scheme.

After a team Christmas party New Jersey Nets guard Micheal Ray Richardson, also known as "Sugar Ray," dropped out of sight for two days before turning himself in to NBA drug counselors for cocaine rehab – his third.

Leonard began to run and work out after Hagler-Hearns, much as he had after Hagler-Duran. Even on the road, he ran and found a gym to hit the bags and jump rope.

Yet, his cocaine habit continued as before. Those close to Leonard suspected something amiss. Trainer noticed that Leonard's visits to his Silver Springs law office were less frequent. Cicero and Getha wondered if an imposter had inhabited their son's body. Leonard's brother, Roger, knew what was wrong. Roger had been drug dependent in the early 1980s and rehabilitated at a Veterans Administration hospital in Washington. Roger joined Juanita's campaign to persuade Leonard to stop.

Late in 1985 Leonard "disappeared" for two or three days with Richard Pryor. The incident alarmed his associates, particularly James Anderson, who understood the depth of Pryor's self-destructiveness. After the Pryor incident Anderson accompanied Leonard to Miami, where they were guests on a yacht. Leonard indulged in yet another round of excess. This time Anderson confronted him.

"I said, very simply, you know, you can do this," Anderson recalled. "It doesn't really affect you but what are people going to say to your children when they go to school. Your father was this great athlete, now he's a drug addict. What about your children? What about Little Ray and Jarrel, what about them?"

Leonard had used cocaine for three years, roughly the time it takes to become addicted to its powdered form. He could not have failed to notice the carnage cocaine had wrought upon the athletic landscape and in general.

One morning he awoke, hung over, and stumbled into the bathroom. In the mirror Leonard saw his once-handsome face bloated. As he stared he experienced his Dorian Gray moment, youth overtaken, as Oscar Wilde wrote, "by a withered, wrinkled and loathsome visage." Self-denial no longer was possible.

"My eyes were bloodshot, my skin was breaking out," Leonard recalled. "I said 'enough.' I started crying actually, and that's when I decided to come back and fight Hagler."

Leonard declined to seek professional help – he wanted no part of a conventional 12-step recovery program such as that in which Roger had rehabilitated. He had in mind something else – a rehabilitation that involved boxing. His 12 steps would be three minutes each.

CHAPTER 12

. . . .

1986: Dinner at Jameson's

"JAMESON'S," A SLEEK NEW steak and chops restaurant in Bethesda, Md., opened to fanfare in mid-January 1986. On hand was its part owner, Sugar Ray Leonard, and his guest, the middleweight champion, Marvelous Marvin Hagler. Both the ex-fighter and the fighter circulated among the crowd of friends, family, and business and media VIPs. Hagler's presence, which lent buzz to the launch, was a coup for Leonard.

Leonard had invited Hagler, and somewhat as a surprise, he had accepted. While Hagler attended as a favor to Leonard, the favor turned out to be more than he intended. This, the first move of Leonard's end game, defined the con and his mark.

Hagler assumed Leonard had reached out in friendship, with no ulterior motives. After his conquest of Hearns, he had become secure enough to let go his envy and resentment of Leonard. After all, Leonard was retired.

Hagler was scheduled to defend against John Mugabi in March.

Leonard and Hagler and their wives, along with Dunlap, Trainer and their wives, relaxed in a private room over dinner and champagne. After dinner, Leonard and Hagler moved off to a quiet corner. Leonard told Hagler he regretted that their bout had never come off.

"What a megabucks fight," Leonard said.

"Yeah, a great show," Hagler said.

Now Hagler, his guard down, confided in Leonard.

"I'm getting tired of the game," Hagler said.

He said he had become more susceptible to cuts and he found it harder to push through his training regimen. Hagler also mentioned that Bertha and his mother had wanted him to retire after the Hearns bout – a parallel to Leonard's own experience. Leonard, one surmises, fixed Hagler with his most effective expression – sincere and sympathetic.

"He kept saying he was not as motivated," Leonard recalled. "And, you know, he's just thinking he's ready to retire right now. And I just heard these things, you know, he's telling me all these things, and I'm saying to myself, this would be the perfect time to fight him.

"I felt that his heart was not into boxing anymore, and that he felt that he'd run his course. He'd done all he could do, and it was time to leave. So I figured that being the case, if I jumped on board, then it would kind of neutralize my five-year inactivity.

"All of these things I heard him say was not from a guy who was still concerned about boxing...and I used that to my advantage."

A month later Leonard asked Dave Jacobs, his long-time trainer, to accompany him to Miami. Leonard and Jacobs had reconciled after their falling-out in 1980. Now Leonard wanted Jacobs to work with him at Angelo Dundee's famed Fifth Street Gym. When Jacobs accepted, Leonard's plan began to take shape.

In March Leonard was a spectator at Hagler's title defense against Mugabi. Ominously, Hagler had been knocked down in practice a few days before the bout.

Mugabi was a far more difficult opponent than Hagler expected, and Hagler showed slippage. He was a fraction slower and weaker. Although Hagler stopped Mugabi in the 11th round, he was cut over both eyes and had his right eye half-closed. Later, Hagler urinated blood for a mandatory urinalysis.

"I remember Marvin being a little disturbed about seeing blood in his urine," recalled Kenny Bayless, an inspector for the Nevada Athletic Commission. Once a physician told him the blood was a result of Mugabi's body blows, and that his urine would return to normal within a day or two, Hagler calmed down.

After the bout, as he walked with martial arts film star Chuck Norris toward Caesars Palace, Leonard said, "I'll get him now." Norris scoffed, "You've been out too long."

Leonard went to the suite of actress Whoopi Goldberg, where the A-list revelers included Michael J. Fox. Leonard eventually settled himself in the oversized bathroom, on the rim of one of the large circular bathtubs, and sipped champagne. Goldberg, Fox, and Dunlap joined

Leonard on the rim of the bathtub, all fully clothed, and happily inebriated.

"I want to fight Hagler," Leonard announced, to general delight.

Leonard had Dunlap dial up Trainer on the east coast and roust him from sleep.

"Mike, I want to fight Hagler," Leonard said.

"Call me when you sober up," Trainer said, and hung up.

Still later, Leonard repaired to a favorite Las Vegas nightclub where he sipped Dom Perignon and chatted with a few reporters. "I can kick Marvin's bleeping butt," he said.

Back in Maryland, Leonard went to see Trainer.

"Michael, me and Hagler, who wins?" Leonard asked.

Trainer looked Leonard in the eye.

"Ray Leonard can't beat Hagler, but Sugar Ray Leonard can."

Leonard recalled the conversation years later.

"When he said that, I didn't understand at first...He was saying that Ray Leonard – the civilian, the businessman, the media personality – couldn't win a fight like that. But if I could get back to being Sugar Ray, I could win."

Now, paradoxically, Leonard needed to be Sugar Ray in the ring, even as he had to reject Sugar Ray out of the ring.

Trainer advised Leonard to not challenge Hagler but to lure him into making a challenge.

"I told Ray, 'From a business standpoint it would be easier for me if you looked reluctant – it's better if Hagler is chasing you,'" Trainer recalled.

On the first of May Leonard was at City Hall in Washington to help raise funds for a sports medicine foundation. Interviewed by Channel 9 reporter James Brown, Leonard could contain himself no longer. Asked about Hagler, Leonard said, "If Marvin Hagler called me I'd consider coming back."

To a *Washington Post* reporter, Leonard said, "If Hagler called me tomorrow, yes (I would fight again). That's why I'm in the gym. If you have his phone number, have him call me up."

Leonard's challenge dominated sports commentary, as columnists and talk radio hosts offered generally critical and dismissive reactions.

"You could hear it all over town yesterday, as if the city had taken a left hook to the gut," wrote Thomas Boswell in the *Post*. "It's a particular kind of grunt you give involuntarily when you hear bad news that's a complete shock yet completely expected, too.

"...From his bald head to his southpaw style to the swift sleep he brought Thomas (Hit Man) Hearns, Hagler is the embodiment of the fighter we don't want Leonard to fight.

"With his middleweight size and love for punishment, Hagler hurts you. He changes you. Permanently."

Hagler reacted like someone who had been duped – again! Worse, he felt betrayed. After he had helped Leonard with his restaurant opening, and had confided his innermost anxieties, now Leonard wanted to fight him. Hagler later said he had been "suckered" by Leonard. "Marvin felt like he was stabbed in the back," said Robbie, his brother.

Two weeks passed without a response. Then, on the "Tonight Show," Hagler replied. "Basically, he has an ego trip or something," Hagler said. "Little jealousy. He's missing the limelight a little. But the way I look at it, I'm just going to sit back and lick my chops. And just wait." He indicated he would make a decision about Leonard within a month.

Hagler, in fact, took 3½ months to decide, during which he raised the possibilities of a rematch with Hearns as well as retirement. Leonard suspected he delayed and equivocated because he enjoyed, for once, his position of control. Yet, there were tangible reasons for his indecision, including those he had confided to Leonard.

Another was that Hagler's marriage was under stress from the same forces – celebrity and temptation – that had shredded Leonard's. During this period his cocaine dissipation allegedly increased.

"My understanding was that he used it straight through the Mugabi bout and was doing it when Leonard came after him," said John Dennis.

Womanizing seemed to be part of the cocaine/celebrity syndrome.

"Marvin had a mindset where he could do what he wanted in marriage," said Betty Whitney, Pat Petronelli's wife. "No question he loved Bertha when he married her and had children. That changed with his celebrity."

Bertha had a volatile temper and was not inclined to be patient with Hagler's infidelity. She was known to throw blunt objects, and to occasionally raise a lump on Hagler's shaved skull. Hagler's indecision, Arum said later, stemmed in part from his reluctance to see Bertha claim half of his huge purse should they divorce. Bertha, who had wanted Hagler to retire after the Hearns bout, now urged him to fight Leonard. "Why don't you go ahead and get that skinny little runt out of the way?" Bertha told him.

As he waited for Hagler's answer, Leonard trained at Palmer Park and occasionally at Dundee's gym in Miami, accompanied by Jacobs and Dunlap. On one of these trips Dunlap confronted Leonard about his comely escort. "You can't have these females – Marvin will kick your ass," Dunlap said. Angered, Leonard ordered Dunlap to ride in the front of a rented limo, and threatened to fire him, but was talked out of it by Trainer. "He's looking after you," Trainer told Leonard.

The rift healed and Leonard began to work out at Dunlap's 10-acre rural spread at Accokeek, Md. Routinely, he showed up in the morning, ran four or five miles, and chopped a tree – a shoulder-strengthening exercise – provided by Dunlap. By noon he was home for rest and late in the afternoon he was at the gym.

In mid-August Hagler was hunkered at his mountain retreat in Bartlett, N.H., without a telephone. Desperate for a decision, Arum, Pat Petronelli, and Betty Whitney set out from Boston, in the middle of the night, to find him. While Arum and Whitney waited at a motel, Petronelli drove up a mountain road, at dawn, to Hagler's secluded house. Hagler was in no mood to see him.

"Marv didn't want it," Petronelli recalled. "He said, 'I'm done. I want to play.' He just didn't want to fight."

Petronelli marshaled his powers of persuasion. He talked to Hagler about his legacy, getting even with Leonard, providing for his family, the unprecedented vastness of the purse, and the chance to make history. "You'll always wonder what would have happened," Petronelli said.

Finally, Hagler let out a deep breath and nodded. "If I fight this one promise me it's all over," Hagler said. "No more."

Word of Hagler's decision reached Leonard at Cosell's plush home on Long Island, at the Hamptons, where he was a guest. When the call came from Trainer, Leonard and Dunlap whooped it up. Cosell was aghast. "No, you're not going to do that," he said.

"Oh yes," Leonard said.

1986: 12 Rounds

The bout was negotiated during a two-month period, mostly over the telephone, with Hagler in New Hampshire, his attorney Morris Goldings in Boston, the Petronellis in Brockton, and Leonard and Trainer in Maryland. But in his Garbo-like seclusion, Hagler refused to put in a telephone. This lent the process a comical aspect.

When he needed to be consulted, Pat Petronelli called Hagler's neighbor, who relayed the question and called back with an answer.

"One day this happened two or three times," recalled Goldings. "Little did we know he had to run up a mountain to do it – nobody knew this guy wasn't next door. Finally, the poor guy said, 'I hope this is the last question – I'm getting exhausted.'"

Leonard had four objectives. He wanted a 12-round distance rather than the "championship" 15-round distance. He wanted a ring no less than 20 feet square – some were 18 feet square – and he wanted 10-ounce attached-thumb gloves rather than 8-ounce. All three conditions mitigated Hagler's presumed advantages of conditioning, strength, and punching power. Lastly, he wanted the fight in Las Vegas, which was odd, given that he had been furious at the scores for his 1981 bout with Hearns.

Most important was the 12-round distance. Though Leonard had needed 15 rounds for two of his major wins – against Benitez and Hearns – he now favored 12. The unspoken reason was the uncertain effect of his three-year cocaine and alcohol binge. Only Leonard knew how much he had indulged, and what his body could sustain.

Two cocaine-related deaths of athletes had made headlines over the summer. University of Maryland All-American Len Bias, chosen No. 2 in the NBA draft by the Boston Celtics, succumbed to cocaine intoxication. Cleveland Browns safety Don Rogers died of a cocaine-induced heart attack. Bias had spent his younger years playing basketball where Leonard learned to box, at the Palmer Park Community Center. Leonard could not but have been affected by Bias' death and wondered about his own physical erosion.

As the talks progressed Leonard came to a realistic assessment of his limits. Urged by Trainer, Leonard had undertaken a series of mock 10-round bouts, complete with scoring judges and referee, against imported sparring partners who, like Hagler, fought left-handed and right-handed. One of the mock opponents, Dwayne Cooper, was a Hagler look-alike. Another, Robert "Boo Boo" Sawyer, had been a Hagler sparring partner. Still another, Quincy Taylor, became a middleweight champion in 1994. In the mock bouts Leonard wore large gloves but no headgear, while his opponents wore headgear and small gloves.

"Ray had four fights so he could see what it was like to fight again," recalled J.D. Brown, the assistant whose job was to bring in sparring partners.

Leonard stopped two of the mock opponents, but two others lasted the 10-round distance. He now had an accurate gauge of his endurance, and knew that a 12-round distance against Hagler was smart.

Initially, Hagler opposed Leonard on all three demands, and most stubbornly on the 12-round distance. He remembered that he needed the 14th and 15th rounds to overtake Duran in 1983.

But Hagler's priorities were financial. Trainer understood this from the outset when Petronelli insisted that Arum handle the promotion, rather than bid it out.

"I said, 'We're in a perfect situation – we're both free agents – let's bid it out and get the best deal we can get,'" Trainer recalled. "But Pat was doing business with Arum. It was disappointing."

Arum offered a large up-front guarantee, and less risk, but his cut of revenues ultimately came out of the fighters' shares.

Leonard and Trainer decided to bargain with cash. Over the course of several weeks they lowered their price. Each step down, they asked for a concession. Eventually, they offered to accept a fixed guarantee and leave Hagler most of the upside from closed-circuit theater and pay-per-view TV revenues. Leonard would get a guarantee of $11 million, plus the bonus revenues from the Washington and Baltimore areas. Hagler would get a guarantee of $12 million, plus the bonus revenues from everywhere else, which were projected at $6 to $7 million. So, from an initial position of near parity, Hagler rose to more than 60 percent, while Leonard dropped to less than 40 percent.

With this "victory" at the table, Hagler agreed to Las Vegas, the larger ring, and larger gloves. But the 12-round distance was the prize, still undecided. This issue, the last sticking point, was settled in mid-October at Goldings' elegant offices on Beacon Hill, in a historic brick building by early–19th century architect Charles Bulfinch. Trainer was there, along with the Petronellis and Goldings.

Trainer made an appeal to Hagler's conscience. At the time the 15-round distance was recognized by the World Boxing Association, but not by the World Boxing Council. Both groups were tainted by corruption, but the WBA had the added taint of doing business with South African boxing interests. At the time, South Africa brutally oppressed its non-white majority through a set of laws known as apartheid. Much of the world had carried out a sports boycott of South Africa since the early 1970s. Arum, who promoted shows in South Africa, was dubbed the "Apostle of Apartheid," although Arum contended that by doing business he encouraged reform.

"Leonard used this brilliant tactical maneuver," Goldings recalled. "You don't want to go with the organization that supports South Africa. He played that card."

Trainer told Pat Petronelli the 12-round issue was "a deal breaker" and that Leonard was prepared to pull out. This was unlikely. Indeed, in an HBO interview after the bout, Leonard said, "He could have said 15 rounds – what could I have done? I couldn't have said anything. He was the champion. I don't think he realized that."

Leonard, who had shunned politics as a matter of business, now positioned Hagler with a political argument. The irony was thick, though lost on Petronelli. He phoned Hagler in New Hampshire and laid out the ramifications. They discussed the possibility Leonard's demand was a bluff.

Hagler decided not to find out. He did not want to call a bluff if it meant being on the side of a pro–South African organization. He might win the hand, but lose his self-respect and reputation.

"Marvin was no dummy," Goldings recalled. "He understood that issue."

Hagler might have insisted on 15 rounds, and absorbed the political heat, if he had felt it absolutely necessary. Duran had been a close call, but four opponents had fallen since Duran. It had been 10½ years since he lost to Willie Monroe – his last defeat. Hagler could scarcely remember losing. Hubris had become the spoiled offspring of his success.

Trainer goaded Hagler's pride.

"You're telling me it's going to take 15 rounds to beat the welterweight," Trainer said. "You've got to be kidding me. Nobody in the world thinks the fight is going to go 12 rounds."

"Marv thought it wouldn't make a difference," recalled Pat Petronelli. "He didn't think Ray could hurt him, and he didn't think he could dance for 12 rounds. Marv thought he would knock him out. The rounds, gloves, and the ring didn't matter."

A third and unspoken reason could have accounted for Hagler's capitulation. He may have decided, as Leonard may have, that fast living had sapped his endurance.

In accepting the 12-round distance Hagler avoided one political pitfall, but stepped into another. The Mexico City–based WBC was closely aligned with promoter Don King. For years Hagler had refused to deal with King, while Leonard had allowed him to co-promote the first Duran bout. If Leonard beat Hagler, King could bid on a rematch. Or, if Leonard won and retired, King could gain control of the middleweight division. If Hagler won, Arum would remain in control.

Hagler's advisors should have been wary of the WBC. Later, when they insisted on a Mexican as one of three scoring judges, they should have been wary.

"Marvin was always battling the system – he had no real political smarts," Emanuel Steward recalled. "He was just a country bumpkin, so to speak, a country boy."

1986: Killing Him Softly

The curtain went up – literally - at New York City's gilded Waldorf Astoria Hotel on November 3, 1986.

It was made of gold tufted satin, and it ascended dramatically above the stage of the Grand Ballroom. Revealed, to the amazed silence of hundreds of media

© 1987 Globe Newspaper Company

Hagler displayed one of his prized belts on the promotional tour more than four months before the bout.

– and the chuckles of a few – were Leonard and Hagler, upon elevated pedestals, side by side. The two warriors stared into the distance as cameras blazed away.

Hagler wore a practical New England suit of dark cloth, with a red tie and gold stickpin. Leonard wore a tapered Italian jacket of white leather – custom made for $1,200 – with a peach vest and taupe tie.

No question which was the tortoise and which the hare.

They posed together for the first time since their contracts had been signed. They did not look at each other or exchange a word, not even a thank-you for the guaranteed $23 million pot they would share. Eventually they sat down at a head table, as the promoter, Arum, took the dais.

"I'm reminded of an old Hebrew prayer," Arum, a Talmudic scholar in his youth, said. "Bless our God who allowed us to see this day."

Leonard spoke first, and instantly waged psychological warfare.

"Before we put on our fight faces," Leonard said, "I want to take the chance to thank Marvelous Marvin Hagler for this opportunity."

Leonard walked a few steps to where Hagler sat, and extended his hand. Hagler ignored it and stared straight ahead. After a few awkward seconds Leonard returned to the dais.

"Apparently he already has his fight face on," Leonard said.

This was the first volley in Leonard's "kill Hagler with kindness" campaign. The idea was to keep Hagler pacified, on the theory that he fought best when angry. Leonard's intention was to praise Hagler, show him respect, and anesthetize his inner beast.

"I never said anything to upset him, because I didn't want to piss him off to make him more motivated to train harder," Leonard recalled. "I was very nice to him...that's reverse psychology."

© 1987 Globe Newspaper Company
Hagler started the publicity tour in Boston in November 1986, but quit after appearing with Leonard in several cities.

Hagler spoke next. His remarks were a transparent effort to conjure enthusiasm. He said he had long anticipated the bout, and had saved "my body, my mind just for this occasion." But his true frame of mind was best revealed by a hint he dropped.

"If this is your last fight, you want to make sure it's a good one," Hagler said. "I'm coming out smoking, physically and mentally."

Soon both fighters embarked on a 12-city promotional tour. One of the early press events was in Boston. Leonard flew in, while Hagler drove up from his home in Hanover, Mass., and arrived 45 minutes late. When he walked in Leonard buttonholed him.

"Marvin, this is a business. You can't be late."

"Yeah, yeah, I got kids," Hagler said.

© Angie Carlino

Comedian Bob Hope, center, thanks Hagler, left, and Leonard, right, for the memory, during the promotional tour, December 1986.

"When you go to work, you go to work," Leonard said.

Hagler nodded and offered no rebuttal. Now Leonard had asserted himself as the more professional.

They promoted the bout in Bethesda, Las Vegas, Los Angeles, and San Francisco. At each stop Leonard praised and complimented Hagler. In Las Vegas, Leonard said,

© Angie Carlino

Marvelous Marvin Hagler, left, promoter Bob Arum,
center, and Sugar Ray Leonard, right, promote their
bout at Caesars Palace, December 1986.

"It's an honor to get in the same ring as the marvelous
one." Then he introduced his sparring partner, the Hagler
look-alike, Dwayne Cooper, whose shaved head evoked
a mirthful reaction from the media. Hagler joined in the
merriment, and insisted he was "better looking" than
Cooper. The more jocular Hagler was, the better Leonard
liked it.

At one event Leonard and Hagler posed together for
a photo. Leonard matter-of-factly took Hagler's fist and
pulled it to his chin. Docile, Hagler stood with his arm
extended.

"Normally, if a guy would take your fists and put it up
to his chin, you'd snatch it back," recalled Pepe Correa,
one of Leonard's trainers. "Hagler never did. And that
gave Ray time to check out what his reach was."

After the San Francisco event, Hagler told Arum, "I
can't take this anymore." He knew the tour had dulled

what little edge he had. Hagler cancelled out of press events in Chicago, Detroit, Houston, Dallas, San Antonio, Atlanta, and Miami.

"Why couldn't he tell me he was going to knock my head off?" Hagler said. "All he kept saying was that he was honored to fight me. I didn't need to hear that."

CHAPTER 13

· · · · · · · · · · · · · · · · · · · ·

1987: Palm Springs and Hilton Head

SPRING IS THE MOST beautiful season on the desert. Tourists came to the Coachella Valley for the soft breezes, flowering plants, blue skies and golf. At the foot of the San Jacinto Mountains, in Palm Springs, lay the Canyon Hotel, where Marvelous Marvin Hagler trained. His workouts became another spring attraction.

After his afternoon session in the tent behind the hotel, Hagler signed autographs and posed for photos. Now in camp for seven weeks, this was how he thanked the 150 to 175 fans that paid $5 to watch him train.

This particular day the autograph line included a middle-aged African American man with dyed gray hair, horned-rim eyeglasses, and a hat pulled down over his forehead. When the man reached the front of his line Hagler assented to his request for a photo without a second thought. The man handed his camera to Lee Samuels, Arum's assistant, and put his arm around Hagler as Samuels snapped the photo.

J.D. Brown flew out that evening and was at Leonard's camp, at the Intercontinental Hotel, Hilton Head, S.C., the next day. Soon he presented Leonard a photo that eventually would be published in Sports Illustrated. More important, he gave Leonard and his trainers a scouting report.

Brown had watched Hagler spar with the identical triplets, Floyd, Lloyd, and Troy Weaver. The Weavers, brothers of former heavyweight champion Mike Weaver, were young pros, athletic and fast. They were supposed to simulate Leonard, and show Hagler lateral movement and speed. They did their jobs well enough that Hagler became frustrated as he chased them.

"They were runners, guys who moved, and he got frustrated," Brown recalled. "He kept saying 'stop moving, come on and fight.' And I thought this is a strategy here."

"The Weavers were out-boxing Hagler," recalled Leonard. "That convinced me I could beat Hagler if I boxed him."

The spy caper was Leonard at his mischievous best, but there was more. While in camp Leonard went to five public schools near Hilton Head and lectured on the dangers of drug use. That he could do so without mentioning his own three-year cocaine binge suggested that his devilish alter ego, Sugar Ray, had awakened to do battle with Hagler.

Leonard undermined Hagler in another way that Hagler, who had quit the promotional tour in December, could scarcely have complained about. With his purse virtually fixed, and Hagler's pegged to audience turnout, Leonard cut back on his media availability.

He gave interviews, with a few exceptions, only after his Monday workout, in the hotel ballroom, in a news conference atmosphere. A few reporters from the Washington area and the largest national media outlets were allowed to interview him in his suite.

Reporters were handed prepared responses to the Four Most Asked Questions, and advised that actually asking them could result in sudden silence. The questions, and paraphrased answers, were: "Why do you want to fight? ("It's the challenge"); "Do you need the money?" ("No"); "Are you concerned about losing your sight?" ("No. I have had the best medical care."); "What does your wife think?" ("She supports me. I love her.")

The Hilton Head camp was set up to minimize distractions. At 3 p.m. about 100 residents and school children from local towns came to watch Leonard train. Autographs were a hit-or-miss courtesy, depending on his mood.

The ring was located in the hotel ballroom until mid-February when it was relocated under a tent on a tennis court. Janks Morton had Leonard fight nine minutes at a crack, against rotating sparring partners. Leonard, who had fought 125 rounds in the six months before camp, fought 125 more between January and the end of March. His punch counts were charted, in short increments, which enabled Leonard to know when he tended to slow down and needed to pick up the pace. Workouts were taped and reviewed, while tapes of Hagler were dissected and studied. "We'd be watching the film and Ray would say, 'Ange, he's gonna throw a right hook,' or 'Ange, he's gonna throw an uppercut,'" recalled Dundee.

Leonard's parents, and a longtime friend, Roland Kenner, cooked his meals. Joe Broddie, Juice Gatling, and his brothers, Roger and Kenny, kept him company. Trainer engaged the media. Juanita visited with their two sons on the weekends; otherwise, Leonard abstained from sex.

Dundee, who in past camps worked just the final two weeks, came for five. J.D. Brown was in charge of six sparring partners. Dunlap, who swore off smoking to set the tone, kept everybody on a military clock, with mandatory running at 6 a.m. They ran on hard-sand beaches, in winter squalls, gray overcast and rain, and gradually, spring sunshine.

"It was one of those camps that was all business," Dunlap recalled. "It was about being in camp – that's what we did."

Leonard chose Hilton Head, not only because Trainer was partial to its golf and the Intercontinental had made an attractive offer, but because South Carolina called to him. Cicero Leonard had grown up near Mullins, S.C. When Cicero went with his son to inspect the Intercontinental, he had remembered his youth and the farm he worked with his father Bidge.

The hotel virtually was unoccupied in early January when Leonard set up camp. Though there were few guests, the hotel staff numbered about 300, most of which, like Cicero Leonard, were working people from small South Carolina towns. The hotel ran an employee shuttle bus to towns as far as three hours away because Hilton Head housing was too expensive.

The staff became Leonard's unofficial booster club, in the absence of his fan base from the Washington-Baltimore area. Leonard built a rapport with the staff that sustained him through a long and rigorous camp. "Everybody jumped through hoops for him – he became family," recalled Thomas Wicky, the hotel general manager.

When it came time to break camp in late March Leonard hosted a party for the employees. He gave watches to a few favorites, passed out typewritten letters of thanks, and posed for photos. The absence of cash tips, however, irked Irving Rudd, Arum's Borscht Belt–ish publicist, who took a dim view of the Leonard camp. Rudd was peeved because he had been accused of spying for the Hagler camp.

Meanwhile, Hagler was in his third camp at the edge of the desert, a long way, in miles and rigor, from Provincetown. The shift from Provincetown to Palm Springs had symbolized Hagler's upward mobility, and the erosion of his spartan ethic. In January, the night before he had flown to California, Hagler had been in a minor car accident in Boston. The time of the accident, 2 a.m., also symbolized Hagler's "upward" mobility. Hagler said his car had slid on ice, but Pat and Goody Petronelli were dubious.

Hagler's camp consisted of the Petronellis, his brother Robbie, and a few sparring partners. Despite the resort setting and the mellowing of his inner Spartan, Hagler retained some monastic habits. He often ate alone in his room, and even watched the Super Bowl alone in his room. He carried his own equipment bag from his suite to the ring under an outdoor tent. As was past practice, Hagler abstained from sex, and demanded abstinence from the others, including the sparring partners.

But there were aspects to his camp that, taken together, suggested Hagler was out of kilter. Most obvious was his exaggerated reaction to a question about Leonard's eye.

"I plan on hurting him – I want to hurt him," Hagler said. "I plan on hurting Sugar Ray Leonard. I want to hurt him bad. I want to smash his eyeball out. I want to knock his head. I want to rip his brains out. Seriously."

Promotional rhetoric had crossed the boundary of bad taste, particularly considering public apprehension over Leonard's eye. It was atypical of Hagler, and suggested deep misgivings about a sensitive issue. One of his earliest opponents, Sugar Ray Seales, a 1972 Olympic gold medalist, had been legally blind since 1983 as a result of boxing, and had spoken out against Leonard's return to the ring.

The eye issue had everybody on edge, including Leonard. Before now, detached retinas had been deemed career ending.

"It was a very emotional time for the boxing industry – to allow this to happen," recalled Duane Ford, then chairman of the Nevada Athletic Commission. "So many people were so prejudiced against a fighter who had a detached retina. It was like saying a guy had AIDS."

The five-member Nevada Athletic Commission, under the scrutiny of Gov. Richard Bryan, had put Leonard through extensive tests in October before it approved the bout by a 3-2 vote.

Lobbied by Nevada, the World Boxing Council convention had overturned its ban on fighters with detached retinas, and sanctioned the championship bout by a single vote.

Still, many opposed the bout, in outspoken terms.

"Whether Sugar Ray wins or loses he will be hurting himself as well as doing great damage to the sport he loves," wrote Jose Torres, chairman of the New York State Athletic Commission, and a former light heavyweight champion.

Dr. Ferdie Pacheco, NBC's "Fight Doctor" and Ali's former physician, wrote, "This match endangers the eyesight of Leonard, as well as his life, and makes a mockery of the credibility of any boxing commission that sanctions it."

Gil Clancy, the trainer-turned-TV commentator, said, "You can't tell me you operate on his eyes and later on he can see fine."

The chairman of Nevada's medical advisory board, Dr. Charles Filippini, resigned in protest over the bout.

Boxing was a $300 million-a-year business in Nevada. Politicians, business owners and athletic commission members understood the potential economic consequences if Leonard were seriously hurt.

"The governor never led me to do it or not to do it," Ford recalled. "The only thing he said to me was, 'Duane, make sure you're right.'"

All of this was nerve-jangling background noise to

both camps. Leonard refused to answer questions about his eye. Perhaps if he had talked openly about it, explained the repair in medical terms, and reassured media and fans, he could have defused the issue. In his silence he encouraged mystery and fear, and left Hagler to deal with it.

"The most important psychological warfare Leonard waged was about his eyes," said Goldings, Hagler's attorney. "He wanted Marvin to have a concern in the back of his mind about blinding him. He knew how decent Marvin was, and how he wouldn't want that legacy."

Hagler's harsh invective continued. Leonard was a "phony," a "copycat," and a "built machine."

"When Ali left, they gave it all to Leonard," he said. "They gave him Ali's trainer. They gave him Ali's style, strategies...He doesn't even have his own name. They gave him Sugar Ray Robinson's name."

Those close to Hagler knew the invective masked a conundrum. Try as he might, he could not objectify Leonard, as he had most other opponents, with the exception of Duran. He had befriended Leonard, and now he could not summon the requisite spleen.

"He didn't have the anger or hate – it just wasn't there," recalled Betty Whitney.

At the outset of his final week at Palm Springs, 13 days before the bout, Hagler did not spar on consecutive days, and his roadwork was reduced. Goody Petronelli explained that Hagler was "too fine" in his conditioning and needed to taper off. Media speculated that Hagler had peaked too early, or had caught a cold and needed rest.

When Hagler resumed sparring it was in private. Hagler and the Petronellis had learned of J.D. Brown's spy mission and were miffed. Hagler's workouts would be closed until the bout, eleven days hence.

At Hilton Head Island, Trainer denied that he or Leonard had knowledge of a spy mission.

Cryptically, Trainer added, "We know exactly what Hagler is doing."

CHAPTER 14

·····················

1987: Every Guest a Caesar

LEONARD ARRIVED IN ANCIENT Rome, aka Vegas, on March 30, a day before Hagler. Both were chauffeured to the front steps of Caesars Palace, where trumpets blared a fanfare, a nubile Cleopatra took their hand, and a costumed emperor intoned, "I, Julius Caesar, extend a royal welcome to one of boxing's legendary champions."

The juxtaposition of casino and stadium, boxers and hustlers, was ever curious. The most Spartan of sports had chosen the most decadent of cities in which to be displayed. Specifically, it had chosen a hotel and casino that was called Caesars, and not Caesar's, because every guest was considered a Caesar. It was a casino where the ceilings were vacuumed at dawn, statuesque blondes and statues of Roman gods adorned the expansive pool, daredevils on motorcycles flew over and into huge fountains, and the Sports Book took nine kinds of bets on a fight.

Caesars was king of The Strip in the last days before

the mega-resorts. This was to be Caesars' 44th world title bout since its first in January 1978, when Roberto Duran stopped Esteban DeJesus, and its most lucrative. The 15,336-seat stadium had sold out in 16 days, at an average ticket price of $513 (high $700 and low $100) for a live gate of $7.9 million. The live gate would be larger than the total gate of the Super Bowl, held two months earlier at the 104,000-seat Rose Bowl in Pasadena, Calif. Another 6,100 seats were sold for closed-circuit viewing in the Caesars showroom. Six other hotels sold 21,500 seats for the closed-circuit telecast.

The population of Clark County (616,000) was three times what it had been in 1967 and one-third what it would be in 2007. It would expand by more than 10 percent when 57,494 hotel rooms were filled before the fight. There were 1,100 credentialed media alone. Before this, the largest media assemblage had been 780 for the Hagler-Mugabi bout. Media came from 31 countries,

© Las Vegas News Bureau

Caesars Palace, circa 1986.

necessitating three translators in the pressroom, located in a pavilion behind the casino and adjacent to the stadium in the parking lot.

The city that billed itself as the Entertainment Capital of the World was wired. Ol' Blue Eyes, Frank Sinatra, was at the Golden Nugget with Jan Murray. Kool & The Gang played Caesars, Willie Nelson the Circus Maximus, and Della Reese the Four Queens. Roseanne Barr, Father Guido Sarducci, Janie Fricke, T. G. Sheppard, Alan King, Redd Foxx, Paul Anka, and Engelbert Humperdinck were at various venues. Nostalgia buffs could catch Sammy Davis Jr. and Jerry Lewis at Bally's. Caesars announced that Jay Leno, who had opened strongly for Patti LaBelle in January, would be brought back as a headliner in the summer. Slot players at the Hilton, on Tuesdays through Thursdays, could win a complimentary pass to see Wayne Newton. A local entertainment columnist, Pete Mikla, wrote, "Barry Manilow dropped by the Crystal Room at the Desert Inn to catch the Suzanne Somers show Wednesday night." Hungry revelers could dine on filet mignon and crab legs for $6.95 at the Maxim Hotel and Casino.

Little of the above mattered to Hagler and Leonard in their final week of preparation, though Hagler seemed more in the spirit of the city, playful and energized. On his first day in Vegas Hagler banged on the door of Johnny Tocco's Ringside Gym, a small and rundown but venerable landmark. "Warden, warden, let me in," shouted Hagler. "I can't take this cruel world anymore."

Johnny Tocco, the crusty 60-something owner, greeted Hagler and helped him set up to train. Hagler had been at Tocco's since his 1979 bout with Antuofermo, and preferred its intimacy to the larger gyms. Tocco, a Hagler favorite, was given a special T-shirt not available to the public. On the T-shirt was a drawing of Hagler, arms raised, with one foot on Leonard's chest. It read: "The Champion. No Mercy."

Hagler wore a hat with the lettering "War II," but in fact his mood was not warlike. He stayed at Caesars, in a suite flanked by rooms occupied by the Petronellis, secluded from the casino but close enough to the Strip for evening walks. One day he and the Petronellis toured the Bonnie Springs Ranch, a local petting zoo and Wild West attraction on the outskirts of Vegas. He petted goats and buffalo and was drawn to the pigeons, his fascination since youth. They viewed a mock hanging at the Old West town, wherein a hooded "victim" was placed in a noose

© 1987 Globe Newspaper Company

Hagler called the Leonard bout "War II." His epic 1985 knockout of Thomas Hearns had been "War I."

upon a platform, and a trap door was released, but a special harness prevented him from actually hanging. "Don't get me near that thing," Hagler cracked.

One evening Hagler and Pat Petronelli walked past Circus Circus – a Strip hotel and casino that featured circus acts – when an elephant was led outside for air. "I want to pet it," Hagler said, and proceeded to do just that, sticking his hand close to the elephant's mouth. When Hagler walked away the elephant followed him for a few steps, until retrieved by its handler.

On April 1 Hagler let himself into Pat Petronelli's suite at 7 a.m. and rousted Petronelli from bed. "Wake up – you got a telephone call," Hagler shouted. "All your horses got out of the corral."

As Petronelli, who raised horses at his Hanover, Mass., home, groped for the phone, panic-stricken, Hagler cackled, "April Fool."

That afternoon, Hagler's relaxed demeanor was on display before the assembled media at Caesars' indoor pavilion. A reporter asked a follow-up question to a reference Hagler had made to Leonard's ego.

Reporter: "When you say Leonard has an ego, does that mean you think you've got what he wants?"

Hagler: "What do you think?"

Reporter: "I know what I think. I want to know what you think."

Hagler: "No, what do you think?"

Reporter: "I think you think so."

Hagler: "Yeah, I think so. That's why I know know what I think – that I think so."

After the laughter died down, Hagler's mood began to

turn. He vowed that he would not be inhibited by Leonard's eye, and declined to reveal his tactical plans, though he hinted, "You don't know – I might out-box him."

An inevitable question about Leonard's greater fame, and whether the fight was an opportunity to turn the tables, awakened his deep, and lately dormant, sense of victimization. Jealousy and sarcasm welled up.

"I remember when Ray was making all the money and Ray was this and Ray was that," he said. "People said I missed out because of the fact that I wasn't colorful enough. I didn't have the charisma; I wasn't marketable. I didn't have the showboating type of personality.

"But look at me now.

"I think he's on an ego trip. He sees me doing very good. Here's all the press, here's all the attention, here's my name in every household. People recognize me as that bald-headed fighter."

Apprised that Leonard's co-trainer, Janks Morton, had predicted he would look like "an amateur" in being knocked out, Hagler bristled.

"How can I look like an amateur when I got more knockouts than he's got fights?" said Hagler. "Just because he won the gold medal and was America's sweetheart doesn't necessarily mean I'm a bum.

"But that's good. I like that – it means they got all the confidence. It means they're going to show up. Don't get 'em all discouraged. I'm trying to keep this man under control so he shows up. Jeez, I got all this money I've got to make."

Meanwhile, Leonard's demeanor was anything but

playful and relaxed. He was quartered in a home at a private country club with Dunlap and a couple of security aides. His parents, who had a room at Caesars, complained that they were not allowed to cook for him. When Leonard asked Tocco if he could train at his gym, he was refused, because he had stood up Tocco a few months earlier, and left him waiting at the gym.

As a result, Leonard trained at the larger but less atmospheric Golden Gloves Gym. His first session was open, and about 100 media watched him spar with Quincy Taylor. Flat-footed and stationary, and markedly thicker through the chest, biceps and thighs, Leonard gave the impression that he might confront Hagler toe-to-toe. Indeed, Leonard toyed with a surprise tactic, to move in on Hagler and cut him up. It lasted until Taylor landed a body blow that made Leonard wince and gasp for air. Somehow, media observers failed to gauge the punch, but Leonard's corner was mortified.

"Ray was knocked out on his feet," J.D. Brown recalled.

Later, the van ride back resembled "a morgue," but, if nothing else, the punch cleared Leonard's head and disabused him of the notion that he could fight Hagler at close range. In succeeding sessions closed to media, Leonard reverted to his strategy of movement and finesse.

The eye issue seemed to rankle him. On his first day in Vegas he was required to undergo another eye exam to satisfy the Nevada commission and governor. The painful procedure, in which a small instrument was inserted behind the orbital rim, put Leonard in a bad mood, even as his left eye passed muster.

Media questions about the eye were inevitable, and further appeared to darken his mood. Whereas initially Leonard calculated that the eye issue might work to his advantage and inhibit Hagler, now he was worried that a premature stoppage by the referee or ring physician could result from heightened concern.

Leonard's mood was on display in his last session with the media three days before the bout. Would Leonard predict how long the fight would go? Was he concerned few fighters had managed successful comebacks after long layoffs? Had he changed as a fighter over the years? To each he responded with a curt "No." A reporter who asked about Leonard's refusal to fight a tune-up bout was referred to sarcastically as "coach." Asked who had been his toughest opponent, Leonard said, "Bruce Finch."

Leonard seemed sour and hostile. But since Leonard's emotions often were calculated, nobody was quite sure, not even his inner circle.

"Don't ever try to read him," said Trainer, the attorney. "It's taken me 10 years to get in his head and I know him only a little bit. Everything he does is for a purpose.

"You'll say, 'Gee Ray, yesterday you're happy and today you're sour.' But that doesn't necessarily mean yesterday he was happy and today he's sour. The guy is hard. Everything is choreographed with Ray."

At the final media session, Leonard dedicated the fight to a New York camp for children with cancer. The idea was to present himself as too humane for Hagler to harm.

"It was all a psych," Trainer said later.

. . . .

CHAPTER 15

1987: April 6

Lou D'Amico had a dream. The slight and bespectacled manager of Caesars Sports Book dreamt he was in the audience at the parking lot stadium. Leonard and Hagler awaited the judges' decision.

"I can see Leonard in the ring and Hagler in the ring," D'Amico recalled. "Then I can see Leonard with his hands up and the crowd going berserk."

D'Amico, then 40, awakened from his dream on the morning of the fight. He scurried into the Sports Book offices, summoned his four supervisors, and related his dream.

"I want to have Leonard going for us in this fight," D'Amico told them.

The supervisors were speechless.

"They looked at me like I had two heads," D'Amico recalled.

Normally, a sports book puts up odds that generate

equal betting on both sides, and collects a modest handling commission. D'Amico proposed shifting the odds to generate more bets on Hagler. If Hagler lost, the Sports Book would pay out less than half of its handle, but if he won it would pay out more than half. In essence, D'Amico wanted the Sports Book to bet on Leonard.

"How is Leonard going to win?" his supervisors asked.

"I don't know," D'Amico said. "I just think he will."

That was how the Caesars Sports Book came to drop its odds on a Leonard victory, from 3-1 to 2½-1.

The rest of Las Vegas awakened to a comfortable spring day, with partly cloudy skies and temperatures headed up to 73.

At 8 a.m. the Nevada physicians Drs. Donald Romeo and Flip Homansky examined Hagler and Leonard and pronounced them fit. They proceeded to the 9 a.m. weigh-in at the pavilion, attended by 1000 raucous spectators. Leonard weighed in first, at 158 pounds, which raised eyebrows among the cognoscenti, because he had never carried that much weight, and it was speculated he had sacrificed speed and movement for strength. Hagler came in at 158½, which was fractionally light for him. Stripped to their underwear, they made brief eye contact, then pulled on their garments and departed.

Not present at the morning events were four others who would play roles in the bout. Richard Steele, of Las Vegas, was the referee. Dave Moretti, of Las Vegas, Lou Filippo, of Downey, Calif., and Jose (Jo Jo) Guerra, of Monterrey, Mexico, were the scoring judges. All three judges were veterans who had worked several championship bouts.

The Nevada Athletic Commission had appointed all four within the last 10 days in a process hidden from public view. The Mexico City–based WBC, the only sanctioning body whose title would be contested, had submitted an initial list of judge candidates. The Nevada commission had selected the three judges from the WBC list, although the commission had latitude to expand the list with local judges. Nevada officials probably added Moretti's name to the initial WBC list, recalled Duane Ford, then the commission chairman.

"You get this list and if you're on the commission you're particular because outside officials can come in and lay an egg and we have to explain," recalled Ford. "You're familiar with an official before you let one come in here."

The two fighters were not permitted a formal veto, though, as a "courtesy," their input was considered. Hagler, who distrusted all things British as a result of his 1980 bout in London, rejected Harry Gibbs, of England, from the initial list. Guerra was appointed instead. Hagler and the Petronellis knew little about Guerra or Gibbs, but they embraced stereotypes that Mexican judges preferred punchers to boxers, while European judges preferred boxers to punchers. Guerra, they believed, would be more amenable to Hagler's style.

Steele, 43, a former Marine and professional (light heavyweight) boxer, had refereed numerous title bouts throughout the 1980s, including Hagler-Hearns. Moretti,

42, who worked in customer service for an association of publishers, had judged title bouts since the early 1980s, notably the Larry Holmes–Gerry Cooney heavyweight match in 1982. Filippo, 62, a metallurgist and a former pro boxer, had judged title bouts for 10 years but was best known for his role as a referee in the *Rocky* films. Guerra, 54, made his living in real estate and had worked 40 title bouts.

Caesars was mobbed throughout the afternoon and early evening, its casino and pool area and sports betting parlor shoulder-to-shoulder with boxing enthusiasts, gamblers, and assorted hustlers. D'Amico estimated that 50,000 people were on the property, including more than a thousand owners of liquor stores in for a convention. Those with tickets, including about 2000 "preferred" customers who were provided comps by Caesars, jostled with those who simply wanted to be close to the epicenter. Scalpers got as much as $2500 for a ticket.

Hagler, wedged between the Petronellis, Robbie Sims, and a couple of security aides, used a service elevator and a delivery entrance to get to his dressing room behind the stadium. Leonard arrived in a van that dropped him almost at the door of his dressing room. Guerra and Filippo, anonymous, made their way from their expense-paid rooms at Maxim's. Steele and Moretti arrived from their local residences.

Celebrities and VIPs filled up the choice seats near ringside. Sinatra arrived with restaurateur Jilly Rizzo and Betty Whitney. Entertainers Billy Crystal, Whoopi Goldberg, Joan Collins, Timothy Hutton, Gene Hackman, Jack

Klugman, Tony Danza, Dolph Lundgren, Gregory Harrison, Telly Savalas, David Brenner, Chevy Chase, and Bo and John Derek were there. The Pointer Sisters, who were to sing the national anthem, settled in near ringside. John Madden, Jimmy Connors, Yannick Noah, Willie Mays, Wilt Chamberlain, John Thompson, Ray Mancini, and Thomas Hearns were present. Security officials tried to restrict paparazzi from clogging up the aisles during the preliminary bouts, with little success. Joan Collins and Bo Derek were favorite targets of the cameras, to their delight.

Hagler and Leonard were in adjacent dressing rooms at the indoor pavilion, separated by a thin plasterboard wall. Sound from both dressing rooms carried into the other, recalled Marc Ratner, the Nevada official who was the inspector in Leonard's dressing room.

"When Ray was getting his hands taped by Angelo Dundee they were yelling through the wall, 'Hagler, you're an old man, you're not gonna win tonight,'" recalled Ratner.

Somebody from Hagler's side pounded on the walls and shouted a retort, which provoked another volley from Leonard's group, led by his brothers, Roger and Kenny. The give-and-take went on for an extended period. Leonard seemed better able to ignore it than Hagler, who was tense. Hagler appeared to hyperventilate at one point, according to what "a reliable source with access" told D'Amico. Steele, the referee, came to both dressing rooms to go over rules and regulations, and to instruct both fighters to "obey my commands at all times."

The judges, Moretti, Guerra, and Filippo, took their seats at the edges of the canvas. Filippo and Guerra were on opposite sides. Moretti was opposite the TV broadcasters, Gil Clancy and Tim Ryan, for the live closed-circuit telecast, and Larry Merchant and Barry Tompkins, for HBO's delayed telecast.

Finally it came time for the atavistic entering of the ring. Everything about it – the robed and hooded specter of the fighters, the "blood scream" of the crowd, the ripe anticipation of violence – suggested an ancient and primitive rite. "You know they're not cheering because they like the two guys," recalled journalist Wallace Matthews. "They're cheering for them to kill each other."

Leonard came first, down an aisle lined by police, surrounded by his entourage who fended off the outstretched hands of fans. In place of a traditional boxing robe, he wore a tapered white satin waist-jacket with red trim, flared sleeves and flared red collar – a fanciful Through the Looking Glass fashion. His face was dark and serious as he inched forward, bobbed up and down, and rolled his shoulders. He clambered into the ring, jabbed and fired combinations at the air, spun backward, punched more air, shook out his legs, and jumped lightly from foot to foot. Then the waist-jacket came off to reveal white satin shorts with red stripes. Red tassels on his shoelaces provided racy accents.

Hagler came next, fronted by Robbie Sims and flanked by Pat and Goody Petronelli. His dark blue robe was traditional, with the hood up over his head, and a white towel wrapped around his chest up to his neck. Edwin

Starr's song, "War," blasted from the stadium speakers, and Hagler's face was partially hidden, which created a chilling effect, as though he were Hooded Death. In the ring Hagler removed his robe to reveal dark blue trunks with white stripes and white waistband. He shook out his magnificent torso, and jumped lightly from one foot to the other. Leonard, meanwhile, prowled from one side of the ring to the other, and nearly brushed shoulders with Hagler, who was anchored near his own corner. They avoided eye contact.

High atop Caesars Palace a high-tech fireworks display exploded into an out-sized American flag as the Pointer Sisters sang the national anthem.

Ring announcer Chuck Hull, a local fixture with a deep voice and a coiffure of gray hair, announced the scoring judges, ringside physicians, and the referee. Then it was time.

"This is the main event of the night," Hull proclaimed. "Twelve rounds of boxing for the WBC middleweight championship of the world.

"Introducing in the blue corner, fighting out of Potomac, Maryland, weighing in at 158 pounds, with a pro record of 33 wins and one defeat with 24 KOs, he is the challenger and former undisputed welterweight champion of the world, Sugar Ray Leonard."

Leonard's introduction ended in a crescendo of boos and cheers. Hull continued.

"And in the red corner from Brockton, Massachusetts, weighing 158½ pounds, his pro record is 62 wins,

2 draws, 2 defeats and 52 KOs, the WBC middleweight champion of the world, Marvelous Marvin Hagler."

Hagler's introduction brought a louder more enthusiastic ovation. The crowd was with Hagler.

Steele summoned the fighters and corner men to center ring. Hagler stared at Leonard while Leonard looked down.

"Okay listen, I gave both of you your instructions in your dressing room," said Steele. "I want to caution you again – obey my commands at all times. Shake hands and good luck."

They tapped gloves and returned to their corners. Angelo Dundee talked to Leonard and smoothed clear grease above and below his eyes. Goody Petronelli spoke to Hagler, who pounded his gloves against his chest, and muttered, "Let's go" over and over.

The corner men cleared the ring. The two fighters shook their limbs and looked at one another. The bell rang for Round One.

CHAPTER 16

1987: Twelve Rounds

Rounds 1 and 2: Leonard

Leonard's sorcery, con, science and salesmanship – his very essence – took hold at the opening bell. Within seconds Hagler was, as referee Richard Steele later described it, "sort of hypnotized."

Gil Clancy: "Hagler is not boxing as a southpaw. I just don't like that at all – why he does that I'll never know."

Hagler started in a right-handed, or orthodox, stance, with his left foot and left hand forward. A rare ambidextrous fighter, Hagler could fight orthodox or left-handed, but he was more effective as a southpaw for the reason left-handed pitchers are effective in baseball – they are less frequently seen. Leonard, who had been confused by ordinary southpaws in the past, expected Hagler to fight as a southpaw and occasionally switch.

"To be honest, it was a rather dumb move," Leonard said later. "If he came in southpaw it would have been more difficult. I would have had to concentrate on my balance more."

Not only was Hagler right-handed, he was cautious. He had vowed to "smash out" Leonard's eye, but instead, he plodded forward at a deliberate pace.

Hagler's cautious start gave Leonard time to get his bearings, calm his nerves, and find a groove. It allowed spectators and judges to exhale, expectations to adjust, and drama to build.

Larry Merchant: "It's very clear Leonard is trying to fight a tactical fight, moving away, flurry, clinching, moving again."

Hagler's down-tempo start in an orthodox stance was curious. The most generous explanation is that he sought a quick knockout, and his right-handed stance was a ruse to confuse Leonard and set up his right hand.

"Marvin was fighting for power," said J.D. Brown, Leonard's "spy." "Marvin would use his right hand for the power punch. He fought from the right-hand side because he was trying to knock Ray out."

But Goody Petronelli later conceded that Hagler abandoned his fight plan.

"That wasn't part of our plan at all," Petronelli recalled. "He just did it. You do things out of natural instinct and he probably didn't even know he went right-handed."

The most plausible explanations come back to the basic and complex psychology between Leonard and

Hagler. Pride, vanity, ego, macho – a testosterone-spiked stew of masculinity – were at stake.

Clancy believed Hagler decided to beat Leonard at his own game, as a boxer, and not a brawler. The hubris that lured Hagler into a 12-round distance may have convinced him he could out-box Leonard.

"He was so overconfident," Clancy said later. "He wanted to show Ray he could out-box him."

Tense in the dressing room, Hagler's judgment in the ring may have been impaired by nerves.

"At one point I did this," Leonard recalled, demonstrating a feint. "And he did that" – he demonstrated Hagler's nervous reaction.

"And I said to myself, 'he's just as scared as I am.' So that kind of neutralized things, it gave me a better feeling, a better footing…because I felt that his nerves were just as jittery as mine."

Absent pressure, Leonard was able to dart and feint and sneak in an occasional punch. At two minutes Hagler switched to southpaw and scored to Leonard's body.

With 30 seconds left, Ollie Dunlap shouted "thirty," from his seat at ringside. On cue, Leonard flurried. His three-punch combination was the most active moment in the round.

"My plan was to keep moving and have my corner yell 'thirty seconds' and then attack with a series of combinations to steal the round," Leonard recalled.

Hagler's response was a half-second late and missed. In the final seconds they grappled and were separated by Steele, who barked, "Don't hold him Ray."

All three judges scored the 1st round for Leonard. The 2nd round was more active, though still tentative. Hagler applied more pressure and worked to Leonard's body, but for long stretches he plodded and boxed at a distance.

Gil Clancy: "Ray has done a psych job on him."

Leonard directed a stream of chatter toward Hagler, according to Steele, the referee.

"Leonard would say 'I told you you couldn't box. I told you you were nothing but a puncher, nothing but a slugger,'" recalled Steele. "The more he did it the more Hagler tried to out-box him."

Hagler did not say much, Steele recalled. But Leonard remembered that he did.

"Hagler was talking to me," Leonard recalled. "He

© Jeff Gale

Hagler lost the first four rounds trying to out-box Leonard.

175

called me a girl. He said, 'Slow down, sissy.' 'Fight me like a man, little bitch.'"

With 30 seconds left Leonard scored with a right hand, and in the final seconds, as they grappled, Leonard landed to Hagler's body.

© Jeff Gale

Leonard's fast hands tattooed Hagler's burnished skull.

Again, all three judges gave the round to Leonard. After two rounds Leonard had thrown 51 punches and landed 29, while Hagler had thrown 54 and landed 11. They were slow rounds, and had they occurred in a club fight, spectators might have lost interest. But in this fight they were important, because Leonard's viability was established. The crowd began to shift toward Leonard.

Barry Tompkins: "People were waiting to see what

Leonard brought to this dance. So far he's brought quite a bit."

Rounds 3 and 4: Leonard

Goody Petronelli sounded annoyed as he smeared grease over Hagler's eyebrows.

"Stay southpaw Marvin," the trainer said. "Loosen up. Let 'em go. Try and get a little movement. You're a southpaw."

In Leonard's corner Angelo Dundee was ebullient.

"Be my man!" said Dundee. "You're making these people take notice – you got 'em crazy. Keep it up. I want you smooth, Baby, Smooth!"

Hagler came out as a southpaw – right-handed stance abandoned – and increased his pressure in the 3rd.. Almost immediately he bounced a right off Leonard's head that caught him off balance, and he commenced to work a battering ram of a jab.

Leonard scored with short punches as Steele broke a couple of grapples. "Work and get out – no holding Ray," Steele barked. Though Hagler was supposed to be stronger, Leonard held his own as they grappled shoulder-to-shoulder, then pushed him off at will.

"Most people won't see this," Leonard recalled, "When the referee is breaking us apart I would throw a little upper cut to his head – nothing hard, but just a reminder. Here, still here. I kept doing that, and that was kind of getting the best of him, too, because now I know that I don't have you physically. But mentally, I have you kind of beaten, in a sense."

At a distance Leonard moved in lateral arcs, as Dundee shouted, "Stick and dip." Smothered by Hagler in the final 30 seconds, Leonard managed a right-left combination before the bell. Now Hagler was visibly frustrated and annoyed.

Gil Clancy: "Hagler is starting to lose his temper – Leonard wanted that. He says you've got to frustrate Hagler."

Moretti and Guerra gave the 3rd to Leonard, while Filippo gave it to Hagler.

Twenty years later Moretti watched the tape and reaffirmed his score for Leonard in the 3rd.

"It was his speed – he threw the sharper more effective punches to me," said Moretti.

Before the bell for the 4th, Hagler stood and slammed his glove against his forehead, as if telling himself either to wake up or fight harder. He came out winging lefts and rights that whistled past Leonard's head, though a couple found their mark. They grappled and Leonard scored on the break. Leonard landed a right low to Hagler's washboard stomach that brought a rebuke from Steele.

Larry Merchant: "There may have been no objective evidence to pick Ray Leonard, but up to this point he has provided subjective evidence that his quickness does befuddle Hagler."

Hagler maneuvered Leonard to a corner but Leonard spun out and landed a combination. Hagler caught up and worked to Leonard's body. Now Leonard wound up his right in the bolo motion and landed it at Hagler's belt line or below, a theatrical punch that brought a roar from the crowd.

Larry Merchant: "It's clear now that Leonard is the more confident fighter. Hagler has let him into the fight, or to put it in a more positive way, Ray Leonard has put himself into this fight."

In the final half-minute Leonard landed a three-punch combination and Hagler worked to Leonard's body. Leonard stuck out his face and wagged it at Hagler, and Hagler, visibly frustrated, had angry words for Leonard.

Gil Clancy: "Hagler is not happy about the showboating but he's going to have to figure out how to do something about it."

Again, Moretti and Guerra gave the round to Leonard, while Filippo scored it for Hagler.

Moretti's explanation: "He moved, he didn't let Hagler hit him and he played with his head, trying to make a mockery of him. He just kept moving and punching."

Referee Richard Steele, 20 years later, remembered his surprise at the first four rounds.

"After the first round I figured Hagler was messing around," Steele recalled. "I would go back to the corner and say 'I guess he's gonna knock him out the next round.' Hagler was a bull of a man – you don't stop this guy. He could take a punch and he could fight 12 or 15 rounds – he never got tired.

"Second round – same way. Third round – same way. By the fourth round I had it figured out. Leonard had sort of hypnotized this guy. Leonard had really got into his head. He was trying to out-box Leonard instead of fighting his fight."

Rounds 5 and 6: Hagler, Leonard

Leonard's trickery and finesse were of little use when his jaw received a heavy blow, as happened in the 5th round. Then, instinct took over.

"When you get hit by Marvin Hagler, his punches are very heavy-handed…like a thud, like a boom," Leonard recalled. "Just think of a piston constantly pounding. It's the wear and tear that eventually takes control."

Fatigue rendered Leonard a flat-footed and vulnerable target in the 5th. Halfway through the round Leonard

© Jeff Gale

Hagler hurt Leonard in the 5th round.

was forced to the ropes, momentarily, for the first time. Though Leonard scored with a couple of right leads, by the third minute Hagler bored in and found his range.

At the 2:30 mark Hagler snapped Leonard's head with a right uppercut – perhaps the most punishing blow of the bout. Leonard's legs buckled momentarily, and he clinched.

Tim Ryan: "That one forced him to grab Hagler, no question about it."

"The uppercut kind of stunned me for a second," Leonard recalled. "I wasn't hurt. It was more 'wow – wake up.'"

Leonard's instinct to clinch may have saved him.

"Marvin never knew he was hurt," recalled Tompkins. "Had Ray stepped back, he probably would have been knocked out."

In the remaining seconds Hagler bulled Leonard to the ropes and landed in his methodical telegraphed fashion.

Larry Merchant: "This is what Hagler wants – a war."

All three judges scored the 5th for Hagler – his only consensus round.

Before the 6th, Dundee's voice was urgent. "Don't lay on the ropes," he told Leonard. "You're trying to load up – don't load up."

The 6th began as the 5th, with Leonard flat-footed and Hagler applying pressure. Hagler scored early with a long right and inside with a left.

Steele cautioned Leonard, "Don't hold him now – work and get out." With his back to the ropes Leonard snapped Hagler's head with a sharp right. The blow slowed Hagler until he maneuvered Leonard into a corner at the two-minute mark. He tried to move in, couldn't solve Leonard's defense, absorbed a sudden flurry, and watched Leonard spin out of reach.

Larry Merchant: "As we wind down the sixth round we remind you that Ray Leonard's eyes have become a non-issue at this point."

In the final three seconds Leonard unleashed the cleanest and most theatrical combination of the round. Virtually even to that point, the round tipped to Leonard, in the view of all three judges.

The phrase, "Leonard stole the fight," could well refer to this round. After Hagler's dominant 5th, he should have won the 6th and gathered momentum. He might have won the 6th if not for the last 15 seconds.

"The first minute Hagler won, then Leonard used the second minute to catch up," Moretti said. "He worked off the ropes real well and scored some good punches. The last 30 seconds he scored the harder punches to pull off the round."

Punch statistics after six rounds had Leonard at 117-for-234 for 50 percent, while Hagler was at 103-for-304 for 34 percent. (Punch statistics are indicators of activity and accuracy, not effectiveness, because they say nothing about the force of a punch.)

Rounds 7 and 8: Hagler

Dundee to Leonard: "Outsmart this guy – you're too smart for this guy."

Petronelli to Hagler: "Rough him up – you're the boss. Keep him backing up – he's weak enough as it is. Throw punches in flurries."

The 7th was fought at medium intensity, as Hagler stalked, closed the distance, and worked to Leonard's body. Leonard was flat-footed, but still an elusive target as he varied the distance, angles and tempo. Both fighters fatigued and found second winds.

Barry Tompkins: "Now you really have the idea that conditioning is going to tell the biggest part of this story tonight."

The pace picked up in the final 30 seconds, after Leonard taunted Hagler with a shuffle. Hagler forced Leonard to the ropes and snuck through a few body blows.

Gil Clancy: "Hagler is landing solid punches and Ray is very tired."

Moretti and Filippo gave Hagler the 7th, while Guerra gave it to Leonard.

Hagler won the 7th by a clear margin, according to Moretti.

"Leonard isn't moving like he was," Moretti said. "Hagler went to the body a lot – he slowed him down with body shots."

Before the 8th Dundee commanded Leonard to stay off the ropes.

Dundee to Leonard: "It looks like he's hitting you even though you're not getting hit. I want you boxing this guy."

Petronelli to Hagler: "Get him against the ropes. Drive him – rough him up. He's all yours, okay?"

The 8th looked much like the 7th, interrupted by a 15-second delay to secure loose tape on Leonard's glove. Once again Moretti and Filippo gave it to Hagler, while Guerra scored it for Leonard.

"One of the closer rounds of the fight, probably," Moretti said. "Hagler just out-pointed him – nothing spectacular. He worked the body well."

Leonard now had clinched a decision on Guerra's card, unless he were knocked down or knocked out. Both still were plausible, which meant that Leonard's lead hardly was secure. Moreover, since round-by-round scores are not revealed during the fight – an archaic tradition – neither Leonard nor Hagler knew if they were ahead or behind.

Round 9: Hagler

Dundee to Leonard: "You going to box for me? Box!"

Petronelli to Hagler: "Brawl this guy. Keep the pressure on. Take his legs away right now."

In the 9th the fight became more than a boxing match, and just less than a street brawl. The 9th was the signature, fought at the fastest pace and highest intensity. One hundred ninety punches were thrown, more than the 165 punches thrown in the memorable 1st round of Hagler-Hearns,

The first minute barely hinted at what was to come. Hagler stalked, scored a "vicious left" to Leonard's body, and blocked a flashy combination. Leonard spun away from the ropes and was warned for holding. At one minute Hagler closed the distance and landed a two-punch combination.

Gil Clancy: "That was the best punch of the fight for Hagler."

At 1:30 Hagler backed Leonard into a corner and methodically worked him over. Both gloves thudded against Leonard from a variety of angles.

Gil Clancy: "He's nailing him now."

Barry Tompkins: "Ray Leonard is hurt in his corner."

None of Leonard's tricks could help him. He could not act, talk or dissemble his way out. He had two options: quit or fight.

"You could see Ray was thinking about giving it up," recalled Emanuel Steward. "Because he could say, 'well, at least I came back and I put on a great show.'"

"He was – bang – hitting me, hitting me, hitting me to the body and to the head," Leonard recalled. "And I said, 'Ray, get out of that corner. Get out of the corner. Fight your way out.'

At the instant when it seemed Leonard must crumble, his gloves came alive. They moved faster than Hagler's, and landed more sharply, and forced Hagler to check his attack. Another flurry forced Hagler to step back, and as he did, Leonard spun out of the corner.

Gil Clancy: "Look at that determination on Ray Leonard! Talk about a champion."

Barry Tompkins: "Now it's Hagler who backs off! The crowd is on its feet."

The round was far from over. Hagler resumed his attack at center ring, and it was there Leonard made another stand, as punches rained down, and up, and across. This second toe-to-toe exchange brought the stadium to a din.

Larry Merchant: "You're seeing two champions go at each other and neither one is giving an inch – two great thoroughbreds. Leonard's ability to take punches from Hagler is astonishing, really."

Hagler's strength and surprising speed prevailed, and again forced Leonard to the ropes.

"Leonard had speed but Hagler stayed up with him," Filippo said. "I differed with people who said Leonard was faster. Hagler was tit for tat with him."

Punches blurred in a crescendo of leather. Both warriors

© Jeff Gale

Hagler went for the knockout in a furious
9th, but Leonard fended him off.

nearly were spent. With 15 seconds to go Leonard took a deep breath and dropped his arms. Hagler hesitated.

Barry Tompkins: "Was that a ploy? He looks tired, but he could be play acting."

Hagler could not be certain, and in his expended state, he was leery of a trap. The action slowed momentarily, resumed, and then, mercifully, the bell ended round 9.

Tim Ryan: "An incredible round!"

As in the previous two rounds, Moretti and Filippo scored it for Hagler, while Guerra gave it to Leonard.

The 9th was not easy to score, Moretti recalled, though he had Hagler ahead through most of it. Leonard's escape from the corner was impressive, but not enough.

"A good round by Hagler," Moretti said. "He hurt him – you can tell when a boxer is hurt. He hurt him when he had him in the corner."

A breathless Lou D'Amico made his way at ringside to his friend, the comic actor Jack Klugman, best known for his TV role as sportswriter Oscar Madison in "The Odd Couple." D'Amico, who had shared his dream with Klugman, kneeled down next to his seat.

"Lou, this is the greatest fight I've ever seen," Klugman said.

Rounds 10 and 11: Leonard
· ·

Now materialized the specter of an outcome decided by three judges. Hagler's inability to stop Leonard in the 9th diminished the likelihood of a knockout. Thoughts turned toward the three men with pencils.

Tim Ryan: "I scored that round for Marvin Hagler, but you've got a lot of emotion involved here. In the minds of the judges it will be hard to separate what they admire in this performance from what is actually happening. A good finish by Sugar Ray Leonard and – who knows?"

The 10th, as could be expected after the frenetic 9th, was slow. Hagler scored with a couple of short uppercuts, Leonard flurried to escape a corner, and flurried again at center ring, without authority. Hagler continued to work Leonard's body. In a grapple, Leonard held Hagler's neck and was cautioned by Steele.

Gil Clancy: "Steele continues to warn Leonard – after a few warnings you have to do something about it."

Indeed, the Petronellis later claimed Leonard was warned 39 times and should have been penalized.

"I was hoping the referee would do something, that they'd take points away from him for all the holding," Hagler said later.

But Steele did not deduct a point from Leonard, as he was empowered to do. The warnings, Steele later explained, were "soft warnings."

"The problem was that Hagler didn't show any kind of rejection – he just let him do what he wanted to do," Steele said. "A fighter normally would do something to show that he did not want to be held. As a referee I would be forced to issue a stronger warning or take away a point. I never got that response out of Hagler."

Leonard's willingness to hold, and Hagler's refusal to complain, underscored the finesse gap between the two.

Leonard's finesse also was seen in the ebb and flow of his attack.

Barry Tompkins: "Ray looks like a tired fighter, but I keep thinking it's a ploy."

Larry Merchant: "I think he's gathering strength for round-stealing flurries...coming down the stretch I think he's going to try to steal these rounds."

Indeed, the 10th, essentially an even round, was "stolen" by Leonard. By now, at least two judges – Guerra and Moretti – were drawn to Leonard's finesse. Both awarded the slow 10th to him, while Filippo gave it to Hagler. The 10th was relatively easy to score, Moretti said.

"It just seemed to me that Leonard's punches were crisper," Moretti said.

The 10th was the third of four rounds on which Moretti and Filippo disagreed. It put Leonard ahead, 6-4, on Moretti's card, and left him one round short of clinching a decision from Moretti.

Before the 11th Dundee told Leonard, "We only got six minutes – keep this sucker turning, baby. Six minutes. Champion, I mean champion!"

Petronelli told Hagler, "He wants to rest. I want two big rounds."

Leonard's showmanship hijacked the 11th. At one point he switched to a southpaw stance, and at another he taunted Hagler with a fake bolo. By now he could read Hagler's rhythm, move in as Hagler reloaded, and move out just ahead of Hagler's punches. At 2:30 Leonard snapped off a clean two-punch combination. In the final 30 seconds Hagler lunged awkwardly and missed what appeared to be an open target, but in fact was Leonard offering his head as a decoy. Leonard flurried at the bell.

Barry Tompkins: "At the moment Marvin Hagler is fighting Ray Leonard's fight."

"Marvin was so frustrated and mad – he was really mad the last three rounds," Steele recalled. "Because he knew he had got sucked into fighting Leonard's fight. He knew he had to get him out of there and he couldn't."

Leonard won the 11th by consensus. Moretti said he gave the 11th to Leonard on the basis of "harder cleaner punches."

"Leonard controlled the round," said Moretti.

Now Leonard had clinched a decision from Moretti and Guerra.

Round 12: Hagler
. . . .

The scorecards were secret. Most spectators believed the 12th would be decisive. Both fighters should have, too, though Leonard later said he suspected he was ahead.

Leonard, slumped on his stool, was nearly depleted.

"Words could not describe how exhausted I was," Leonard recalled.

Steele remembered, "Leonard was very tired, because the last half of the fight, Hagler really took it to him."

Dundee exhorted Leonard to summon his final reserve of energy. "Deep breaths, c'mon baby," shouted Dundee. "Stand up. Three minutes. New champion! New champion!"

As though touched by an electric prod, Leonard snapped alive. From his gut came a primal yelp

"Yeh!" He jumped off the stool, arms upraised.

Oddly, Hagler's corner was low-key. Goody Petronelli knew Hagler needed a big round, and possibly a knockout, to win. But his voice and emotional pitch were flat.

"It's the last round – he's trying to win rounds by flurries," Petronelli said. "There's a lot riding on this here. Don't stop until he's down."

Gil Clancy: "Goody Petronelli is in the corner talking like it was a 15-round fight. I would have been a little more emotional if I was in his corner."

Tim Ryan: "I think Hagler has to realize that sentiment is going to have to be with Leonard and he's going to have to knock him out to retain his title."

Gil Clancy: "That's not what they're telling him in his corner. They're talking to him like it's an IBM meeting or something – no emotions."

Leonard moved to center ring. At the bell he extended his gloves to tap with Hagler's in the traditional gesture of sportsmanship. Hagler held back, until Steele guided him toward Leonard and ordered him to tap gloves.

The 12th was theater, as first Leonard, then Hagler, played to the judges. Hagler stalked, and Leonard backpedaled and glided in lateral arcs, just out of range. At one minute Hagler forced Leonard to the ropes and slammed his body with two hard lefts. By now Leonard's response was predictable – he flurried to Hagler's head and spun away. As Leonard danced at center ring, the crowd came to its feet and chanted, "Sugar Ray, Sugar Ray."

Gil Clancy: "You know who the crowd thinks is winning this fight."

Tim Ryan: "Ray Leonard is having fun in there now – what a story."

Leonard mugged and wiggled his right glove in the air. Hagler mimicked him. The two fighters had words and made faces at one another. Leonard unleashed a shuffle. They grappled, Leonard held Hagler's head, and Steele barked, "Let him go Ray."

With 20 seconds left Leonard's back was to the ropes again. Hagler banged at his body, and Leonard flurried softly to Hagler's head.

Ten seconds remained when Hagler ripped a solid left to Leonard's ribs. Leonard "patty-caked," as Moretti recalled it, and Hagler slammed home two more thudding lefts. Then came the final bell, not a second too soon for Leonard.

Barry Tompkins: "How do you like it? How do you like it?"

The parking lot stadium was in bedlam. For the last time the three judges marked their scores. After their pencils stopped moving, Leonard dropped to his knees and was hoisted up by Janks Morton and Ollie Dunlap. Hagler, arms upraised, broke into a kind of nervous shimmy or boogaloo that was out of character and place. The Petronellis, Duane Ford recalled, "told him to knock it off."

Moretti and Guerra gave the round to Hagler, while Filippo gave it to Leonard. The final punch figures had

Leonard at 306-for-629 (49 percent), and Hagler at 291-for-792 (37 percent).

Leonard made his way across the rapidly populating ring to Hagler. The two fighters hugged and Leonard pecked Hagler on the cheek. They exchanged a few words that soon would become the object of minor controversy.

Then Leonard climbed atop a strand of the ropes, raised his arms to the crowd, and awaited the decision.

Larry Merchant: "Both fighters think they won the fight."

Split Decision

The stadium quieted for Chuck Hull's announcement at center ring.

"Ladies and gentlemen, here is the decision of the judges. We have a split decision."

Groans and boos coursed throughout the stadium.

"Judge Lou Filippo scores it 115 Marvin Hagler 113 Ray Leonard.

"Judge Jo Jo Guerra scores it 118 Leonard 110 Hagler.

"Judge Dave Moretti scores it 115-113, for the winner by a split decision, and new..."

The noise drowned out Hull. Leonard, poised on the strand of rope, held his arms aloft, shouted, and beamed his million-dollar smile.

Hagler shook his head and flicked a hand, as if to say, "Bullshit." Robbie Sims consoled him, but Hagler's expression hardened with the realization. Victimized, again.

Lou D'Amico climbed into the ring and hugged Dundee. His dream, and the split decision, yielded a $300,000 bulge for Caesars Sports Book.

Merchant buttonholed Leonard and asked him if he could have lasted in a 15-round fight.

"My heart was in the fight – I would have pushed it no matter what," Leonard said. "This was a great accomplishment for me. A lot of people didn't think I could do it – you didn't – for good reason."

Tapping his heart, Leonard said, "What it was all about was what was in here. I hope they don't say Marvelous Marvin Hagler's talent had eroded. I beat a guy who was as determined as he was in the past."

Moments later, Merchant held a microphone up to Hagler and asked if he thought he had won.

"I did win the fight, no doubt about it, " Hagler said. "After the 4th round I took the fight, kept it going, made him fight every second of the way. I kept the pressure on. He didn't hurt me, that flurry stuff didn't mean anything. I'm in Vegas, you know. He stole it. He knows he lost it, everybody knows he lost it."

"Would you consider a rematch?" Merchant asked.

"I don't want to think about that," Hagler said. "I don't think it's fair."

"Were you surprised at the pace he sustained?"

"That's all he had to do – anybody who goes the distance with me… I gotta tell you Larry, I'm the greatest. I proved I'm the true champion. He didn't knock me down, didn't hurt me at all. C'mon. I just can't believe it."

Hagler moved to exit the ring. From behind Leonard tapped him on the shoulder in a poignant scene captured by HBO's camera.

"Marvin, Marvin," Leonard said.

Hagler glanced sideways at Leonard.

"It wasn't fair," Hagler said.

"We're still friends," Leonard said.

"It's not fair."

"But we're still friends?"

Hagler turned to leave.

"It was a good fight," Leonard said.

Hagler glanced back. He said something inaudible about "Vegas," and added, "You gave me a good fight."

Leonard reached for Hagler's right hand with his left. Their hands clasped for a moment, and then Hagler pulled away.

Later, at the pavilion, before the assembled media, Hagler aired his version of their first exchange of words, just seconds after the final bell.

"Leonard told me himself, 'You beat me,'" said Hagler. "And I was so happy, man, I knew I beat him. And then when they take it away from me like that, it's hard to believe."

Leonard later claimed Hagler misunderstood him.

"I said 'You're still a champion to me,'" said Leonard. "I would never lie to Marvin."

CHAPTER 17

· · · · · · · · · · · · · · · · · · · ·

1987: The Cause of Emotion

HAGLER LEFT THE PAVILION and crossed the parking lot toward the hotel. Thirsty, he spotted a beer truck at a loading dock. "Hey man, can I have a beer?" he asked the stunned driver, who recognized him at a glance. "Sure Marvin, have all you want," he was told. Hagler shouldered a case, thanked the man, and disappeared into the hotel.

Leonard rode on the shoulders of his security chief, James Anderson, through a cheering casino at Caesars. He had lost 13 pounds, and was weak and dehydrated, but wanted to soak in the acclaim. At the coffee shop he ran into Emanuel Steward.

"Who do you think won?" Leonard asked.

"To be honest with you, I had Hagler by a point," Steward said. "But the fact you did what you did puts you on a whole other level – I have so much more respect for you."

The next morning Leonard bought a $15,000 Piaget watch at a hotel boutique.

That same morning the Hagler camp retaliated against Guerra and Moretti.

Pat Petronelli told media that Guerra "should be put in jail" for giving 10 rounds to Leonard and 2 to Hagler. His statement implied Guerra had committed a crime, though no crime actually was charged or uncovered, unless being human, with feelings and preferences, is a crime. Petronelli had no way of knowing that as a young man, in the mid 1950s, Guerra had lived in Chicago. There, he held a factory job and boxed as an amateur at a local gym. One day Sugar Ray Robinson, training for a comeback bout against Ralph "Tiger" Jones, came into the gym and asked for a sparring partner.

"He wanted to pick up speed," Guerra recalled. "The trainer, George Gainsford, said to me 'You're fast – do you want to help him a couple of rounds?' And I said, 'Sure, he's my idol.'"

That was how Guerra came to spar two rounds with the boxer who created the mold – and nickname – for Leonard. If Sugar Ray Robinson was Guerra's "idol," it stands to reason that Sugar Ray Leonard exerted a strong emotional pull on him. That was human bias in its most innocent non-criminal form. Leonard had only to give Guerra a plausible cover to exercise his bias.

In the face of criticism, Guerra refused to apologize or voice regret. "Leonard out-punched Hagler, outsmarted him, out-boxed him," Guerra said.

The irony was that the Petronellis had insisted that

Guerra replace Harry Gibbs, the English judge chosen initially. They seemed to have forgotten that Gibbs had voted for Duran over Leonard in their first bout in 1980. Gibbs later said that he had scored Hagler an 8-4 winner over Leonard.

That same morning Bob Arum phoned Duane Ford, said, "I think the fight was fixed," and voiced "concerns" about Moretti, who gave 7 rounds to Leonard and 5 to Hagler. Ford alerted the office of Nevada Attorney General Brian McKay, who launched an investigation.

The month-long investigation cleared Moretti, who passed a lie detector test. It turned out Moretti had judged a bout in Norfolk, Va., in late March and had flown back to Las Vegas with Billy Baxter, the manager of one of the fighters. Baxter, a prolific local gambler, had talked to Moretti about partnering as boxing promoters. Baxter also had let Moretti know that he had placed a sizeable wager, of at least $30,000, on Leonard. Baxter's relationship with Leonard was such that he had helped arrange for the private home he used before the bout.

Moretti's actions were not criminal, but it stands to reason that Baxter, a potential business partner, exerted a strong emotional pull on him. Leonard had only to give Moretti a plausible cover to exercise his bias.

The attacks on the two judges served Hagler's and Arum's interests – the more dubious the decision the greater the impetus for a rematch, should there be one. But they also reflected the controversy over the decision. The debate began almost the instant it was announced. In a poll taken by *Newsday* of 25 ringside observers, 12 thought Hagler won, 10 scored it for Leonard, and three had it a draw.

A sampling of opinion, spoken and written, for Hagler:

Eddie Futch, trainer to several world champions: "I thought Hagler had a slight edge, probably by a few points. He was the champion and he made the fight with his aggressiveness."

Ray (Boom Boom) Mancini, former lightweight world champion: "Hagler definitely won the fight. Doesn't body punching count for anything anymore? Leonard wasn't doing anything in there but showboating."

Bob Verdi, *Chicago Tribune*: "They gave Leonard points for befuddling Hagler, making him look awkward, for taking Hagler's punches without splintering. Hagler was judged for what he should have done, not what he did. So astonishing was Leonard's imitation of himself that judges paid to be objective became accomplices to Leonard's filigree."

Steve Kelley, *Seattle Times*: "Alibis and sour grapes are as much a part of the fight game as blood and bluster. You listen to excuses, you wade through the sour grapes and you forget them. But last night was different. Marvelous Marvin Hagler was robbed."

Hugh McIlvanney, the *Sunday Times*: "This was showboating raised to an art form, and the brilliance with which it was sustained was a tribute to Leonard's wonderful nerve, which is cut from the same flawless diamond as Ali's...But, however much the slick ploys blurred the perceptions of those on the fevered sidelines, they never broke Hagler...he had enough to press on through his early frustrations and throw the superior volume of hurtful punches. I'm convinced Hagler won the fight; a draw, and the retention of the title, was the very least he deserved."

A sampling of opinion, spoken and written, for Leonard:

Mitch Albom, *Detroit Free Press*: "Fighters speak with their bodies, and in the final rounds Monday night Hagler's said defeat, he had been stumped, stymied, tripped up by light punches and fast footwork and psych job that he knew was coming. And that must have been the worst part. Like a man who can stay awake no longer, Hagler closed his eyes and found his old nightmare – right in front of him. 'I knew this would happen,' he mumbled at one point."

Jim Jacobs, historian and fight manager: "I thought Ray won clearly. He mixed technical skills with intestinal fortitude and Marvin Hagler got old before my eyes."

Fred Klein, *Wall Street Journal*: "The name of the sport is boxing, and on Monday night here Ray Charles Leonard showed why. He gave Marvelous M. Hagler a little this and a little that and a lot of air. When it was over he had Hagler's cherished middleweight championship belt. If Marv had worn a wristwatch into the ring, Leonard would have lifted it, too."

Tony Kornheiser, *Washington Post*: "He'd come like a cat burglar, stealing the crowd and the championship from Hagler. Hagler had advertised a war, and Leonard had obliged. But they weren't reading from the same manual. Hagler fought conventionally, attacking and pursuing straight ahead from a position of strength. Leonard, recognizing his inferior numbers, hit and ran, tantalizing and tormenting Hagler by fighting a thinking man's war."

Jim Murray, *Los Angeles Times*: "He didn't just outpoint Hagler, he exposed him. He made him look like a guy chasing a bus. In snowshoes. Marvelous Marvin Hagler should have put stamps on his punches. He kept aiming them at places Sugar Ray had left much earlier in the evening."

Among those who scored it a draw were Merchant, Dave Anderson of the *New York Times*, and Greg Logan of *Newsday*.

The debate was academic, of course. Leonard was the winner, and the object of public acclaim. Americans who knew little about boxing knew plenty about underdogs, and America's fondness for underdogs reached across its history. Leonard was likened to the New York Mets of 1969, Elvis Presley, Hank Aaron, Jimmy Carter in 1976, the fictional Rocky Balboa, and even the Founding Fathers.

"We are a people who admire the person of limited attributes who fights back," Indiana University sports psychologist Eugene Levitt told *USA Today*. "That appeals to the American soul...the little man overthrowing the big man."

"People have a hero again," said humorist Art Buchwald, who watched a closed-circuit telecast outside Washington, D.C. "Sugar Ray was an underdog. Everybody was worried about his eye. Everybody was worried he couldn't fight. Hagler looked ugly. Sugar Ray looks like somebody you'd adopt. You like the boy-next-door to win."

Leonard won because he tapped into the zeitgeist, as an underdog and as an actor. Indeed, McIlvanney likened boxing judges to theater critics reviewing an actor's performance while "making the pseudo-scientific adjustment of putting their impressions into figures."

"No one has ever understood the boxing judge as reviewer of theatre better than Sugar Ray Leonard," McIlvanney wrote; "...the overriding priority for him appeared to be the manipulation of official minds."

The third judge, Lou Filippo, who gave 7 rounds to Hagler and 5 to Leonard, summed it up. On HBO, a few days later, Filippo was asked if judges tend "to watch the guy who is doing the unexpected."

"That's absolutely right," Filippo said. "Everybody had their eye on Leonard. He causes the emotion."

CHAPTER 18

· · · · · · · · · · · · · · · · · · · ·

1987: Vanished

LEONARD'S MAGIC WAS POWERFUL, indeed – it made Hagler vanish. He vanished from the ring, never to fight again. For months after the fight, he vanished from his family and friends, almost literally. In seclusion he brooded and wept.

Not even his record payday could cheer him. The bout had grossed about $77 million, with close to two million closed-circuit customers, and about 80,000 (out of a potential 700,000) home pay-per-view buys. Leonard's share came to just under $12 million, while Hagler's came to about $18.5 million, an upgrade from his first purse of $50. The money should have cushioned his disappointment, but his mood grew darker by the day.

Pat Petronelli struggled to describe Hagler's fragile emotional state and finally settled upon "funk."

"Marv is in a funk," Petronelli said. "He's not himself."

Leonard returned to Washington and was greeted by 1000 fans at National Airport. A few days later Merchant interviewed him for HBO's delayed telecast. By now Leonard was annoyed with efforts to cheapen his victory. He had been through this before, when Duran's "No Mas" stained his triumph in 1980.

Thus, when Merchant asked Leonard what "stuck out most" about the fight, his response was the verbal equivalent of a low blow.

"The most surprising thing that sticks out is that the fight was relatively easy," Leonard said. "I was able to hit Hagler with shots I would have hit an average guy who was a 12th or 15th contender. I'm not taking away from Hagler but he was more susceptible to punches than I anticipated."

Merchant pointed out that Hagler was perhaps the only "long-time" champion to lose his title by such a close decision, to which Leonard responded, "I don't think it was split. I beat him fair and square, decisively. I think it was unanimous."

Leonard's comments could not have improved Hagler's mood, if indeed he heard them. In late June 1987 Hagler and Bertha legally separated after she told a Massachusetts court he had pushed her out of the house and thrown a boulder at her car.

Days later John Dennis reported on Channel 7 in Boston that Hagler had fallen into "widespread alcohol and drug abuse" and that friends and family members had sought a medical intervention.

Hagler came to the Channel 7 studio and denied he

used drugs. "He said 'You're wrong, I'm not doing this stuff,'" Dennis recalled. "He had the worst head cold you ever saw. His nose was running and he had a Kleenex in his hand. He sat and blew his nose and wiped his eyes. He was denying a coke problem while he had one in front of us. He said he had allergies."

Hagler admitted to Dennis that the loss to Leonard was on his mind. "I've been trying to keep from getting down," he said on-air. "I still think I won the fight, but I realize life has to go on and I still have to grow."

A rematch was widely anticipated, simply because a market existed, perhaps more fertile than the initial market. The bout had been that good, and the outcome that controversial. In a rematch both fighters reasonably could expect to divvy up $25–30 million.

But Hagler was ambivalent. Before the bout he had vowed it would be his last. Minutes after he lost he had hinted at a rematch conspiracy when he said, "they want me back, they want a rematch with Leonard and this is how they done it."

Leonard was coy. He, too, had said the bout would be his last. He had said his objective was to beat Hagler, and that he did not want "a career."

Both fighters waited for the other to reach out. Then in late May Leonard announced his fifth "retirement," which few who had followed his career took seriously. Leonard may have thought his ploy would motivate Hagler, or increase his own leverage. Instead it reminded Hagler of being a prop at Leonard's "retirement" in November 1982, and he recoiled at the prospect of being manipulated again. His lukewarm interest in a rematch waned by the end of 1987, and he gravitated to Italy, where he had offers to act in films, and where he could forget Leonard.

Leonard's "retirement," indeed, was a ploy. Early in 1988 he tried to open talks with Hagler.

"Ray would call me and say 'Get the rematch,'" Trainer recalled. "I'd make another call. They would say 'Great,' and then I wouldn't hear anything.

"Ray wanted Hagler again. Goody wanted it. Pat wanted it. Hagler never wanted it. It baffled Ray."

Hagler announced his retirement in June 1988 while in Ravenna, Italy, for a Robbie Sims bout. He had just finished his first film, *Indio*, in which he played a tough Marine called Sergeant Iron.

"My heart says yes but my brain says no," Hagler told an NBC TV audience. "Boxing has been good to me, but Leonard only wants to play games. It would take at least another year before we could fight, so I'm going to say goodbye to boxing, retire and go into the movies."

Leonard's career became an extended anti-climax. Never again did he fight at the level he attained against Hagler. He beat a Canadian journeyman, Donny Lalonde, for 168-pound and 175-pound titles in November 1988. He was generously awarded a draw against Hearns in an over-ripe rematch in June 1989, and he easily decisioned a 38-year-old Duran in their third meeting in December 1989. Terry Norris drubbed him in a 12-rounder in 1991, and Hector Camacho won by TKO in five rounds in 1997. He was 40 when he lost to Camacho, bereft of speed, power and reflexes.

Leonard separated from Juanita in 1988 and they divorced in 1990. By this time Leonard had met his second wife-to-be, Bernadette Robi, the daughter of Paul Robi, one of the Platters, and the ex-wife of Lynn Swann, the former Pittsburgh Steelers wide receiver.

In June 1990 a final effort by Leonard, Trainer and Arum to lure Hagler into a rematch failed, as Hagler turned down a $15 million offer. "It is finito," Hagler said, in the language of his adopted country.

Later that year Leonard and Hagler found themselves in the same crowded ballroom of an Atlantic City hotel for an event honoring the best fighters of the 1980s. Leonard kept an eye on Hagler and eventually approached him. When Leonard came closer, as if to embrace, Hagler put a firm hand to his shoulder. Without a word Hagler turned and walked away.

"That guy hates me – he really still hates me," Leonard told a reporter.

Late in March 1991 Juanita's sealed divorce deposition was leaked to the *Los Angeles Times*. In the lurid court record Leonard was described as a cocaine user prone to fits of domestic violence. The day the story appeared Leonard called a press conference, at the Washington Touchdown Club, and apologized for his "childish" and "stupid" behavior, which he said occurred between 1983 and 1986.

"So I stand here ashamed, hurt," Leonard said. "I stand here and think about my parents, my ex-wife, my kids, people who care for me, my fans...and I can never erase the pain or the scars that I have made through my stupidity, through my selfishness. All I can say is that I'm sorry, but that's not enough."

Leonard explained how he had stopped using cocaine without help.

"It took Ray Leonard to tell Sugar Ray, 'Hey, you aren't the same person...unless you want your life to be screwed up, you better straighten your life up,'" he said.

The remarkable public confession, in which Leonard rebuked his alter ego, inadvertently opened a new window on his victory over Hagler. The challenge and comeback had been steeper and more perilous than the public had known. In light of Hagler's reported problems, it retroactively injected cocaine as an unknowable wild card into the competitive equation.

Caesars invited Leonard, Hagler, and other celebrities to a 30th anniversary party in September 1996. By then Hagler had met his second wife-to-be, Kay Guarino, a native Italian. Hagler and Guarino were approached by Hearns and told that Leonard wanted to talk about a business proposal involving all three fighters.

"Tommy, you tell him he wants to talk to me, he can talk to me, but you gonna go into business with him?" Hagler replied.

Hearns came back moments later with Leonard in tow.

"Marvin, I just want to talk about business," Leonard said. "We could make a lot of money. Me, you and Tommy."

"You want me to go into business with you?" Hagler said. "I don't think so."

"We can make a lot of money doing it again, Marvin. We don't have to get hurt. We don't have to do that."

"Don't get hurt? That's what I'm about Ray. I'm about hurt. We fight – it's about hurt. I don't play that way."

Hagler looked at Leonard and Hearns, and said, "You guys gotta get a life," and walked away.

In September 1999, at the Mandalay Bay in Las Vegas, Leonard and Hagler attended Oscar De La Hoya's controversial loss – his first in 32 pro bouts – to Felix Trinidad by majority decision. The next day they crossed paths in a lobby. Leonard was in a playful mood; Hagler was not.

"Marvin, can you believe Oscar lost the fight?"

"Yeah, it happened to me, too."

"Really?" said Leonard. "When?"

The new millennium did not soften Hagler's animus. When they were thrown together, at boxing functions, Hagler stayed as far away as possible from Leonard.

"I was at an event with Marvin and Ray and Tommy," recalled Emanuel Steward. "Naturally, the photographers wanted the three of them together. Marvin would not stand next to Ray. He made it so that Tommy was between them."

Hagler, in a 2002 interview with ESPN, demanded that Leonard publicly concede he lost.

"I'm going to wait for the day when he freely admits that 'I really lost that fight – I appreciated that the referees or whatever granted me the decision but I really didn't win the fight,'" said Hagler. "That's what I want."

Early in 2006 Steward and Hagler sat down over

drinks. Delicately, Steward asked Hagler why the rematch never came off. Hagler's response took Steward aback.

"Because I got fucked," Hagler said.

Steward did not ask again.

"You can see why that fight couldn't be made," Steward said. "He's just too bitter.

"I don't think I've ever known a fighter that was so upset with the result of a fight that 20 years later the feeling is still as strong. The fire hasn't dimmed at all."

Nothing had changed by the autumn of 2007, more than 20 years after the bout, as Goody Petronelli, now 85, sat behind his desk at his Brockton gym and described the depth of Hagler's bitterness.

"Marv will take it to his grave," said Petronelli.

Epilogue

. . . .

IN THE COCAINE-ADDLED, JUNK bond '80s, Leonard and Hagler gave us a fable, and themselves a permanent place in boxing lore. Both are elevated among the all-time greats, Leonard a step higher.

As much as his career, Hagler is remembered for his exit. He quit, at the age of 32, after losing to Leonard, and declined multi-million-dollar offers to fight again. He was one of a few champions – Rocky Marciano being another – to quit with his health intact and money on the table.

"Marvin Hagler did a lot of good things by walking away," said Flip Homansky, a Nevada physician who worked the bout. "He walked away at the peak of his health, and I think a lot of our younger fighters could learn a lesson from him."

Hagler's abrupt exit was an oddity, to be sure, but also a natural outgrowth of his career.

"People say he shouldn't be so bitter, but let me tell

you something," said Emanuel Steward. "That chip on his shoulder is what made him a good fighter."

Leonard was larger than life, and sometimes smaller.

In the summer of 1983 Leonard sailed to England on the *QE II* with a Canadian film crew at work on a documentary about him. Princess Margaret and Bob Hope were aboard, and a formal black-tie dinner was thrown. In tuxedoes, Leonard and his bodyguard, James Anderson, made their way to a sparkling men's room, where an attendant handed out towels and accepted tips. But a problem arose after Leonard and Anderson washed their hands – neither had money for the tip box.

"So the guy turned his back to hand another guy a towel," Anderson recalled, "and Ray reached into the change thing, picked it up, and dropped it back in there."

The attendant turned around as change cascaded into the tip box.

"Oh, thank you very much, Mr. Leonard."

"No problem," Leonard said, and returned to the dinner with Princess Margaret and Bob Hope.

This wasn't about stinginess. By most accounts Leonard was a generous man who once wrote a spur-of-the-moment $250,000 check to Grambling, supported relatives and friends, and helped strangers in need.

This was about Leonard feeding his inner con, if just a tiny hors d'oeuvre. This was the same impulse that shaped his strategy against Hagler, and created a timeless classic. As the bout is Leonard's legacy, so is his devilish persona.

Steve Farhood was editor of *KO* magazine from 1980

to 1997, and of *The Ring* magazine from 1990 to 1997. He oversaw coverage of hundreds of championship fights, but none stirred his readers as much as Leonard-Hagler.

"I got more mail on the fight and the decision than any fight in all my years of editing," Farhood said. "I continued to receive mail on the decision years after the fight."

Dave Moretti, the "swing" vote, is never far from the fight.

"Twenty years after the fight it's still the one most people ask me about," Moretti said. "Did Leonard really win?"

The same is true of Jo Jo Guerra, the judge who "wasn't there," yet never escaped from it.

"They made me famous," said Guerra. "Wherever I go, that's the fight people want to know about."

Leonard, in a 2005 interview, said he often is reminded of the bout by everyday fans.

"Even to this day, in New England or wherever I go, his fans will come up to me and say, 'Ray, we like you, but Hagler beat you.' To this very day."

Its enduring appeal may stem from the potent alchemy of opposites. Before the bout Promoter Bob Arum theorized that their personalities were reflected in other athletes, teams, places, politicians, and "ordinary" citizens.

"Everyone and everything is either Hagler or Leonard," Arum wrote in the *Las Vegas Sun*.

Lawrence Taylor and the New York Giants were Hagler; John Elway and the Denver Broncos were Leonard. Most quarterbacks were Leonard, while linebackers and defensive linemen were Hagler.

The Boston Celtics and Larry Bird were Hagler; the LA Lakers and Magic Johnson were Leonard.

California, Florida, Texas, and Arizona were Leonard, while Massachusetts, Pennsylvania, Alabama, Oklahoma, and New Mexico were Hagler. Nevada suffered from a "split personality"; Reno was Hagler, Las Vegas was Leonard. New York City was too cosmopolitan to fit into either category, but the rest of New York was Hagler.

Democrats were Hagler and Republicans were Leonard, with exceptions. Of the Republican presidential hopefuls, Sen. Robert Dole and former Sen. Paul Laxalt were Hagler, while Democratic candidates Gary Hart and Jesse Jackson were Leonard.

On fight night, Arum concluded, "The Haglers and Leonards in the vast audience will be rooting like mad for that fighter representing the personality category each fan identifies with."

The metaphors of 1987...

Leonard was Hollywood, the catwalk, sushi, desktop computing, and the future. Hagler was Main Street, a 30-year mortgage, a burger with fries, a factory that closed, and the past.

...are different today, but the same.

Leonard is an Internet search engine, a hedge fund, and high-definition plasma TV. Hagler is bumper-to-bumper in the morning commute, a windowless cubicle, and late fees on a credit card that never is paid down.

Leonard was who we dreamed of being, Hagler was who we are.

No matter that Leonard was not who or what he

appeared to be. Leonard's magic was in the seductive vision he represented.

Two judges voted for Leonard, one for Hagler. The outcome said as much about our culture and desires as about the fight.

Leonard and Hagler gave us a "marvelous" fight and something more – a looking glass.

"Every time I watch it," said Steele, the referee, "it gets closer."

Appendix

. . . .

Notes on Scoring: Three Perspectives

Jo Jo Guerra had one perspective on the fight. Dave Moretti had a second, and Lou Filippo a third. Each of the 15,000-plus eyewitnesses and two million closed-circuit viewers had a perspective as well. But only those of the scoring judges – Guerra, Moretti and Filippo – mattered.

Absent a knockout a bout enters the realm of subjective interpretation and bias. Judges aspire to apply "objective" criteria, defined as clean punching, defense, effective aggression, and ring generalship. The objective criteria, however, are notoriously subjective, defy consistent interpretation, and invite bias.

If three judges agree on the winner of a round, consensus affirms their view. If all three see it the same way, it can be assumed to be fair.

In this fight the three judges agreed on five rounds: 1, 2, 5, 6, and 11. Those rounds provided a relatively clear winner and allow for relatively "objective" description.

The other seven rounds, 3, 4, 7, 8, 9, 10, and 12, failed consensus. They challenge objective description and represent the crux of the disputed split decision.

The scores of Moretti and Filippo reflected a shared perspective. Moretti gave 7 rounds to Leonard and 5 to Hagler, while Filippo gave 7 to Hagler and 5 to Leonard. In a close fight, absent a knockdown or even a conspicuous blow, their scores were logical and reasonable.

(Under Nevada's 10-point system, a fighter gets 10 points for winning a round, and 9 points for losing a round, unless he is knocked down, in which case he gets 8 points or 7 points. If a round is scored even, both fighters get 10 points. The Nevada Athletic Commission discouraged "even" rounds, and none were scored.)

Guerra, however, awarded 10 rounds to Leonard and 2 to Hagler, a score that indicated a dominant performance by Leonard. Guerra's score was vilified by the Hagler camp, ridiculed by the media, and rued by the top Nevada boxing official, Duane Ford, who said, "I was wondering where a judge was."

In defense of his score, Guerra said, "I voted with the majority."

In other words, he got the winner right, but the margin of victory wrong. Guerra's score can be put into perspective. If the three scores are viewed on a continuum, with Guerra's 10 rounds for Leonard representing the far range, and Filippo's 5 rounds for Leonard representing the near range, then Moretti's 7 rounds for Leonard nearly falls in the middle. Guerra's score was almost as close to Moretti's as was Filippo's.

Moretti was the swing vote. Had he awarded one more round to Leonard, Filippo's score would have been more divergent than Guerra's. Had he awarded one more round to Hagler, his score would have been 6-6, and the bout would have ended as a draw.

In the final tally, Guerra disagreed with Moretti on three rounds, and with Filippo on five rounds. Moretti and Filippo disagreed on four rounds. The lack of consensus highlighted the subjectivity of the scoring system, and the closeness of the bout.

The irony of boxing is that when a gloved fist does not decide the outcome, a pencil does.

Notes on Sources and Acknowledgments

· ·

As THE *Boston Globe*'S boxing writer from 1979 to 1988 I covered Sugar Ray Leonard and Marvelous Marvin Hagler. Material for this book began with my own articles and recollections, and from *Globe* archives.

The archives of numerous other newspapers were accessed via electronic database and microfilm. Accounts from the *Brockton Enterprise* were helpful in reconstructing the early phase of Hagler's career, as were the *Lowell Sun*'s coverage of the 1973 Golden Glove nationals and *Boston Herald* archives.

Washington Post archives helped reconstruct Leonard's career. Leonard's early phase was sketched in Alan Goldstein's book, *A Fistful of Sugar*. The archives of *Sports Illustrated*, *Newsweek* and *Time* magazines filled in details, as did the *New York Times* and *Los Angeles Times*.

Several books provided insight: Leroy Ashby's *With*

Amusement For All, Dave Kindred's *Sound and Fury*; David Remnick's *King of the World*, Christian Giudice's *Hands of Stone*; Hugh McIlvanney's collection of columns, *The Hardest Game*; Jim Brady's *Boxing Confidential*; Joyce Carol Oates' *On Boxing*; and Irving Rudd's *The Sporting Life*.

Video recordings of HBO, CBS, and closed-circuit telecasts were essential.

Research included interviews with Leonard, Hagler, Emanuel Steward, Mike Trainer, Charlie Brotman, Pat Petronelli, Goody Petronelli, Betty Whitney, Tony Petronelli, Angie Carlino, Steve Wainwright, Morris Goldings, John Dennis, Dave Moretti, Lou Filippo, Jo Jo Guerra, Richard Steele, Duane Ford, Lou D'Amico, Prentiss Byrd, Bert Sugar, William Gildea, Dave Kindred, Thom Greer, Jose Sulaiman, Steve Farhood, Royce Feour, J.D. Brown, Pit Perron, Thomas Wicky, and Rich Rose.

Ollie Dunlap, who interviewed with me at his Toronto home, offered his photo collection, as well as hospitality.

Angie Carlino, who doubled as photographer for Hagler and the Massachusetts Bay Transportation Authority, was kind enough to excavate a storage bin for his vintage shots.

Access to ESPN's vast interview archives was generous and instrumental. From Worldwide Leader transcripts came words of Leonard, Hagler, Bob Arum, Juanita Wilkinson, Roger Leonard, Kenny Leonard, Getha Leonard, Sandra Leonard, James Anderson, Barry Tompkins, Larry Merchant, Angelo Dundee, Jose Pepe Correa, Janks Morton, Dave Jacobs, Russell Peltz, Peter DeVeber, Flip

Homansky, Marc Ratner, Kenny Bayless, Teddy Atlas, Al Bernstein, Lee Samuels, William Nack, Ron Borges, Wally Matthews, and Mike Katz.

I owe special thanks to ESPN's Vince Doria for his help and editing eye, and to former colleagues Leigh Montville and Ian Thomsen for their contributions, on the tee and off. Royce Feour, the dean of Las Vegas boxing writers, was gracious and encouraging. Many years ago Mike Katz mentored me on the boxing beat, and for that I remain grateful.

The Caesars Palace publicity staff of Debbie Munch, Ken Langdon, and Kathy Silvas extended professional courtesy.

Longtime friend and gifted photographer Stuart Cohen whipped the photos into shape. Friend and boxing aficionado Peter McNerney made available his cache of articles. Longtime friend and clinical social worker Bruce Freeman offered moral support and comic relief.

I am indebted to the robust boxing journalism that flourished in the 1970s and 1980s, exemplified by Red Smith, Dave Anderson, Mike Katz, Pat Putnam, Ed Schuyler, Bill Nack, Dick Young, Jim Murray, Bob Waters, Vic Ziegel, Rich Hoffer, Wally Matthews, Greg Logan, Mike Lupica, Mike Marley, John Schulian, Bob Verdi, Leigh Montville, George Kimball, Ron Borges, Bert Sugar, Hugh McIlvanney, Colin Hart, Frank Deford, Jane Leavy, Tom Boswell, Dave Kindred, Bill Gildea, Jerry Izenberg, Bill Lyon, Tom Cushman, Mark Kram, Mark Kram Jr., Jon Saraceno, Joe Gergen, Thom Greer, Elmer Smith, Jack Fiske, Ralph Wiley, Phil Berger, Rich Hofmann, Al Goldstein, Jim Fenton, Tim Horgan, Tom Archdeacon, Mike O'Hara, Dave Kindred, Royce Feour, Bill Reader, Steve Farhood, Dave Bontempo, Joe Carnicelli, Randy Gordon, and Flash Gordon.

I wish to thank my publisher, Jeremy Solomon, who took a sporting chance, against the odds, and my editor, Linda Weinerman, whose eyes were fresh and discerning.

On a personal level, my two children, Nora and Alex, feigned interest and offered loving support.

My wife, Alison Arnett, a career newspaper journalist, endured several iterations, and executed the first edit. Her vow "for better or worse" was stretched above and beyond. My respect for her is exceeded only by my love.

Index

INDEX

INDEX

About the Author

Steve Marantz covered boxing during the Leonard-Hagler era for the *Boston Globe*. As a beat and investigative reporter, columnist and feature writer, he covered sports, politics, and government for the *Kansas City Star, Trenton Times, Boston Globe*, WHDH-TV, *Sporting News*, and *Boston Herald*.

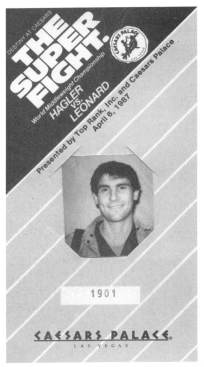

Author's press pass for the Hagler/Leonard fight

He is a researcher for ESPN Content Development and co-founder of SportsMediaGuide.com, which explores the art and craft of sports coverage.

Marantz grew up in West Virginia and Nebraska and graduated from the University of Missouri School of Journalism. He and his wife, Alison Arnett, raised their children, Nora and Alex, in Swampscott, Mass.

Sugar Ray Leonard's split-decision victory elevated him a step above Marvelous Marvin Hagler among the all-time greats and won bragging rights to an era.